MCA

Microsoft® Office Specialist (Office 365 and Office 2019)

Study Guide

PowerPoint Associate Exam
MO-300

Eric Butow

SYBEX®
A Wiley Brand

Copyright © 2021 by John Wiley & Sons, Inc., Indianapolis, Indiana

Published simultaneously in Canada

ISBN: 978-1-119-71846-8
ISBN: 978-1-119-71848-2 (ebk.)
ISBN: 978-1-119-71847-5 (ebk.)

For general information on our other products and services or to obtain technical support, please contact our Customer Care Department within the U.S. at (877) 762-2974, outside the U.S. at (317) 572-3993 or fax (317) 572-4002.

Wiley publishes in a variety of print and electronic formats and by print-on-demand. Some material included with standard print versions of this book may not be included in e-books or in print-on-demand. If this book refers to media such as a CD or DVD that is not included in the version you purchased, you may download this material at booksupport.wiley.com. For more information about Wiley products, visit www.wiley.com.

Library of Congress Control Number: 2021934205

TRADEMARKS: Wiley, the Wiley logo, and the Sybex logo are trademarks or registered trademarks of John Wiley & Sons, Inc. and/or its affiliates, in the United States and other countries, and may not be used without written permission. Microsoft and PowerPoint are registered trademarks of Microsoft Corporation. All other trademarks are the property of their respective owners. John Wiley & Sons, Inc. is not associated with any product or vendor mentioned in this book.

SKY10026760_050421

To my family and friends

Acknowledgments

I have many people to thank, starting with my literary agent, Matt Wagner. He connected me with Sybex to write this book and managed our relationship well. Next, I want to give a shout-out to my excellent editing team: Gary Schwartz, Barath Kumar Rajasekaran, Christine O'Connor, and Senior Acquisitions Editor Kenyon Brown.

And, as always, I want to thank my family and friends for their everlasting support. I couldn't write this book without them.

—Eric Butow

About the Author

Eric Butow is the owner of Butow Communications Group (BCG) in Jackson, California. BCG offers website development, online marketing, and technical writing services. Eric is a native Californian who started working with his friend's Apple II Plus and Radio Shack TRS-80 Model III in 1980 when he lived in Fresno, California. He learned about programming, graphic design, and desktop publishing in the Fresno PC Users Group in his professional career, and when he started BCG in 1994.

Eric has written 38 other technical books as an author, co-author or, in one case, as a ghostwriter. Most of Eric's works were written for the general book market, but some were written for specific clients, including HP and F5 Networks. Two of his books have been translated into Chinese and Italian. Eric's most recent books are *Programming Interviews for Dummies* (For Dummies, 2019) with John Sonmez; *Ultimate Guide to Social Media Marketing* (Entrepreneur Press, 2020) with Jenn Herman, Stephanie Liu, Amanda Robinson, and Mike Allton; and *Instagram for Business for Dummies, Second Edition* (For Dummies, 2021) with Jenn Herman and Corey Walker.

Upon his graduation from California State University, Fresno in 1996 with a master's degree in communication, Eric moved to Roseville, California, where he lived for 13 years. Eric continued to build his business and worked as a technical writer for a wide variety of businesses, from startups to large companies, including Intel, Wells Fargo Wachovia, TASQ Technology, Cisco Systems, and Hewlett-Packard. Many of those clients required their technical writers to know Microsoft PowerPoint, which Eric has used since the early 1990s. From 1997 to 1999, during his off-time, Eric produced 30 issues of *Sacra Blue*, the award-winning monthly magazine of the Sacramento PC Users Group.

When Eric isn't working in (and on) his business or writing books, you can find him enjoying time with friends, walking around the historic Gold Rush town of Jackson, and helping his mother manage her infant and toddler daycare business.

About the Technical Editor

Kristen Merritt is an experienced technical editor who has reviewed books for several publishers, including Wiley and Microsoft Press. Kristen spent 12 years in technical sales, and she is currently employed as a digital marketer.

Contents at a Glance

Contents

Table of Exercises

Introduction

Welcome to this book about becoming a Microsoft Certified Office Specialist for Microsoft PowerPoint, which is a component of the Microsoft 365 suite of productivity applications to which you can subscribe. You can also use this book with the one-time purchase version of PowerPoint, which Microsoft calls PowerPoint 2019.

Microsoft 365 allows you to use the different versions of PowerPoint on many platforms, including Windows, macOS, iOS, iPadOS, and Android. You can even use the web version of PowerPoint on the free online version of Microsoft 365. This book, however, talks about using the most popular version of PowerPoint on the most popular operating system, which happens to be PowerPoint for Microsoft 365 running on Windows 10.

You may already know about a lot of PowerPoint features by working with it, but no matter if you use PowerPoint for your regular slideshow tasks, or if you're new to the application, you'll learn a lot about the ability that PowerPoint gives you to create all kinds of slideshows.

Who Should Read This Book

If you want to prepare to take Exam MO-300: Microsoft PowerPoint (PowerPoint and PowerPoint 2019)—which will help you become a certified PowerPoint specialist and hopefully increase your stature, marketability, and income—then this is the book for you. Even if you're not going to take the exam, but you want to learn how to use PowerPoint more effectively, this book will show you how to get the most out of using PowerPoint based on features that Microsoft believes are important for you to know.

What You'll Learn from This Book

What you learn in this book hews to the topics in Exam MO-300, because this book is designed to help you learn about the topics in the exam and pass it on the first try.

After you finish reading the book and complete all the exercises, you'll have an in-depth understanding of PowerPoint that you can use to become more productive at work and at home (or in your home office).

Hardware and Software Requirements

You should be running a computer with Windows 10 installed, and you should have Power-Point for Microsoft 365 or PowerPoint 2019 installed and running too before you dive into this book. Either version of PowerPoint contains all the features that are documented in this book so that you can pass the exam.

How to Use This Book

Start by taking the Assessment Test after this introduction to see how well you know PowerPoint already. Even if you've been using PowerPoint for a while, you may be surprised at how much you don't know about it.

Next, read each chapter and go through each of the exercises in the chapter to reinforce the concepts in each section. When you reach the end of the chapter, answer each of the 10 Review Questions to test what you learned. You can check your answers in the appendix at the back of the book.

If you're indeed taking the exam, then there are two other pedagogical tools that you can use: Flashcards and a Practice Exam. You may remember flashcards from when you were in school, and they're useful when you want to reinforce your knowledge. Use the Flashcards with a friend or relative if you like. (They might appreciate learning about PowerPoint, too.) The Practice Exam will help you further hone your ability to answer any question on the real exam with no worries.

How to Contact Wiley or the Author

If you believe you have found an error in this book, and it is not listed on the book's web page, you can report the issue to our customer technical support team at support.wiley .com.

You can email the author with your comments or questions at eric@butow.net. You can also visit Eric's website at www.butow.net.

How This Book Is Organized

Chapter 1: Creating Presentations   This chapter introduces you to managing presentations, including how to modify slide masters, handout masters, and note masters; change presentation options and views; configure print settings for your presentation; configure and present slideshows; and prepare presentations for collaboration with others.

Chapter 2: Managing Slides   This chapter follows up by showing you how to insert slides, including from Word and other presentations; insert Summary Zoom slides; modify slides, including inserting slide headers and footers; as well as how to order and group slides.

Chapter 3: Inserting and Formatting Text, Shapes, and Images   This chapter shows you how to format and apply styles to text in a slideshow; insert links; insert and format images; insert and format graphic elements, including shapes and text boxes; as well as order and group objects on slides.

Chapter 4: Inserting Tables, Charts, SmartArt, 3D Models, and Media   This chapter tells you how to insert and format tables, charts, SmartArt graphics, 3D models, audio and video clips, and screen recordings into a slideshow.

Chapter 5: Applying Transitions and Animations   This chapter covers how to apply and configure transitions between slides, animate content within a slide, and set timing for slide transitions.

Interactive Online Learning Environment and Test Bank

Learning the material in the *MCA Microsoft® Office Specialist (Office 365 and Office 2019) Study Guide: PowerPoint Associate Exam MO-300* is an important part of preparing for the exam, but we also provide additional tools to help you prepare. The online TestBank will help you understand the types of questions that will appear on the certification exam.

The Sample Tests in the TestBank include all of the questions in each chapter as well as the questions from the Assessment Test. In addition, there is a Practice Exam containing 50 questions. You can use this test to evaluate your understanding and identify areas that may require additional study.

The Flashcards in the TestBank will push the limits of what you should know for the certification exam. The Flashcards contain 100 questions provided in digital format. Each flashcard has one question and one correct answer.

The online Glossary is a searchable list of key terms introduced in this Study Guide that you should know for Exam MO-300.

To start using these to study for the exam, go to www.wiley.com/go/sybextestprep and register your book to receive your unique PIN. Once you have the PIN, return to www.wiley.com/go/sybextestprep, find your book, and click Register, or log in and follow the link to register a new account or add this book to an existing account.

Exam objectives are subject to change at any time without prior notice and at Microsoft's sole discretion. Please visit the Exam MO-300: Microsoft PowerPoint (PowerPoint and PowerPoint 2019) website (docs .microsoft.com/en-us/learn/certifications/exams/MO-300) for the most current listing of exam objectives.

Objective Map

Objective	Chapter
Section 1: Manage presentations	
1.1 Modify slide masters, handout masters, and note masters	1
1.2 Change presentation options and views	1
1.3 Configure print settings for presentations	1
1.4 Configure and present slide shows	1
1.5 Prepare presentations for collaboration	1

Assessment Test

1. In what menu ribbon do you add a bulleted or numbered list?

    A. Design

    B. Home

    C. Insert

    D. Slide Show

2. When you want to add a slide from another presentation, what option do you select in the New Slide drop-down list?

    A. Duplicate Selected Slides

    B. The custom theme slide

    C. Reuse Slides

    D. Slides from Outline

3. What are the two ways to configure animation paths in a slideshow? (Select all answers that apply.)

    A. Motion paths

    B. The Animation Pane

    C. The Transitions ribbon

    D. Morph

4. What are the four table row and column insertion types?

    A. Row, Column, Header Row, First Column

    B. Top, Bottom, Left, Right

    C. Above, Below, Left, Right

    D. Left End, Right End, Top, Bottom

5. What do you have to do to add information into a slide?

    A. Add a theme

    B. Add a new slide master

    C. Modify the slide master content

    D. Click in a placeholder area

6. Why do you add a link to a slide? (Select all answers that apply.)

    A. To link to an email address

    B. To connect with a website

    C. To create a new slide

    D. To link to another slide

7. What options do you have when selecting a footer? (Select all answers that apply.)

   A. Date and Time

   B. Company

   C. Don't Show on Title Slide

   D. Copyright information

8. When you want to add a SmartArt graphic, which menu option do you click?

   A. Design

   B. Slide Show

   C. Insert

   D. Home

9. What view do you use when you want to see thumbnail-sized images of slides?

   A. Notes Page

   B. Reading view

   C. Slide Sorter

   D. Outline view

10. What are some of the audio and video formats that you can add into a PowerPoint slideshow? (Select all answers that apply.)

    A. MPEG

    B. OGG

    C. WAV

    D. FLV

11. From what sources can you insert an image? (Select all answers that apply.)

    A. Office.com

    B. Web images

    C. Stock images

    D. JPEG format images

12. What slide content can you animate? (Select all options that apply.)

    A. Text

    B. 3D Models

    C. Pictures

    D. SmartArt graphics

13. What menu option do you click to print a slideshow?

    A. Home

    B. View

C. File

D. Design

14. What can you move when you modify the order of slides? (Choose all that apply.)

   A. Master slides

   B. One or multiple slides

   C. Sections

   D. Layouts

15. What is the term for the effect that occurs when you move from one slide to another in your slideshow?

   A. Animation

   B. Morph

   C. Transition

   D. Effect

16. What are the three ways to change the text appearance in a shape or text box? (Select all answers that apply.)

   A. Convert to SmartArt

   B. Text Direction

   C. Text Effects

   D. Align Text

17. When you change your mind immediately after setting a new slide background, what do you do? (Select all answers that apply.)

   A. Change the slide background back to what it was.

   B. Press Ctrl+Z.

   C. Close the slideshow without saving it and then reopen it.

   D. Click the Undo icon.

18. What are some of the elements that you can modify within a chart? (Select all answers that apply.)

   A. Numbers

   B. Legend

   C. Gridlines

   D. Lines

19. Your boss wants you to create a slideshow that runs automatically for the big tradeshow coming up. What do you do to set the transition time between each slide?

   A. Set the duration in the Animations ribbon.

   B. Use the tools in the View ribbon.

    C. Select the After check box in the Transitions ribbon.

    D. Change the theme in the Design ribbon.

20. How do you get a good idea where PowerPoint places objects in a slide? (Select all answers that apply.)

    A. An object snapping to a point within the slide

    B. Gridlines

    C. The mouse pointer

    D. Guides

21. After you add a transition, how do you add an effect to it?

    A. Change the theme in the Design ribbon.

    B. Change the view to Slide Sorter in the View ribbon.

    C. Click Effect Options in the Transitions ribbon.

    D. Add a new slide in the Insert ribbon.

22. What are the types of custom slideshows that you can create? (Select all answers that apply.)

    A. Simple

    B. Multi-Slide

    C. Hyperlinked

    D. Timing

23. Where can you find 3D models to insert into a slide? (Select all answers that apply.)

    A. The Insert ribbon

    B. Stock models

    C. On your computer

    D. The Illustrations section in the Insert ribbon

24. Where do you modify the slide order in the PowerPoint window?

    A. The Design ribbon

    B. Right pane

    C. The View ribbon

    D. Left pane

25. What are the two ways that you can keep others from editing a slideshow? (Select all answers that apply.)

    A. Mark the slideshow as final.

    B. Email the users to tell them not to edit the slideshow.

    C. Add a slide that tells the users not to edit the slideshow.

    D. Use a password.

Answers to Assessment Test

1. B. You add a bulleted or numbered list using the tools in the Home ribbon. See Chapter 3 for more information.

2. C. Select Reuse Slides from the bottom of the drop-down list to select a slide from another slideshow to insert into your slideshow. See Chapter 2 for more information.

3. A, D. You can add motion paths to animate an object within a slide and use the Morph feature to animate objects between slides. See Chapter 5 for more information.

4. C. You can add a row above or below a selected table cell, as well as a column to the left or right of the selected cell. See Chapter 4 for more information.

5. D. When you want to add information into a specific slide, you click in the appropriate placeholder area, such as the area for the slide title, and then add your text and/or object(s). See Chapter 1 for more information.

6. A, B, D. PowerPoint allows you to add various types of links, including to an email address, website, and another slide within your slideshow. See Chapter 3 for more information.

7. A, C. You can add a date and time and slide number, and you can also choose not to show the footer on the title slide in a slideshow. See Chapter 2 for more information.

8. C. Click the Insert icon to add a SmartArt graphic in the Illustrations section in the Insert ribbon. See Chapter 4 for more information.

9. C. The Slide Sorter view shows thumbnail-sized images of all slides in your slideshow for your review. See Chapter 1 for more information.

10. A, C. You can add audio and video MPEG files, WAV audio files, and many other audio and video file formats. See Chapter 4 for more information.

11. A, C. You can insert images from Office.com, PowerPoint stock images, and images stored on your computer. See Chapter 3 for more information.

12. A, B, D. You can animate text, 3D models, and SmartArt graphics in a slide. See Chapter 5 for more information.

13. C. Print a document by clicking the File menu option and then clicking Print in the menu on the left side of the File screen. See Chapter 1 for more information.

14. B, C. You can move one or multiple slides as well as all slides in a section. See Chapter 2 for more information.

15. C. A transition is the effect that happens when the slideshow moves from one slide to another. See Chapter 5 for more information.

16. A, B, D. You can convert text to a SmartArt graphic, change the text direction, and change the text alignment. See Chapter 3 for more information.

17. B, D. You can press Ctrl+Z or click the Undo icon in the Quick Access Toolbar. See Chapter 2 for more information.

18. B, C. You can change the legend, view gridlines, and modify many other elements in a chart. See Chapter 4 for more information.

19. C. After you select the After check box in the Transitions ribbon, you can set the time for each slide transition. See Chapter 5 for more information.

20. B, D. You can get visual cues of where PowerPoint places objects in a slide with gridlines, guides, and rulers. See Chapter 3 for more information.

21. C. After you add a transition, click Effect Options in the Transitions ribbon to view all effects that you can set for that transition. See Chapter 5 for more information.

22. A, C. You can create a simple custom slideshow that you create for a specific audience, as well as a hyperlinked slideshow that contains links to custom slides for different audiences. See Chapter 1 for more information.

23. B, C. When you add 3D models in the Illustrations section in the Insert ribbon, you can add stock models installed with PowerPoint or 3D models stored on your computer. See Chapter 4 for more information.

24. D. You modify the order from within the list of thumbnail-sized slides in the left pane. See Chapter 2 for more information.

25. A, D. PowerPoint allows you to mark a slideshow as final and add a password to your slideshow file. The latter is more effective at keeping reviewers from editing your presentation. See Chapter 1 for more information.

Chapter

1

Creating Presentations

MICROSOFT EXAM OBJECTIVES COVERED IN THIS CHAPTER:

✓ **Manage presentations**

- Modify slide masters, handout masters, and note masters
    - Change the slide master theme or background
    - Modify slide master content
    - Create slide layouts
    - Modify slide layouts
    - Modify the handout master
    - Modify the notes master
- Change presentation options and views
    - Change slide size
    - Display presentations in different views
    - Set basic file properties
- Configure print settings for presentations
    - Print all or part of a presentation
    - Print notes pages
    - Print handouts
    - Print in color, grayscale, or black and white
- Configure and present slide shows
    - Create custom slide shows
    - Configure slide show options
    - Rehearse slide show timing
    - Set up slide show recording options
    - Present slide shows by using Presenter View

- Prepare presentations for collaboration
    - Mark presentations as final
    - Protect presentations by using passwords
    - Inspect presentations for issues
    - Add and manage comments
    - Preserve presentation content
    - Export presentations to other formats

Greetings, and welcome to this Microsoft Office Specialist Study Guide for PowerPoint, which is designed to help you study for and pass the MO-300 Microsoft PowerPoint (PowerPoint and PowerPoint 2019) exam and become a certified Microsoft Office Specialist: PowerPoint Associate. If you have your favorite beverage on your desk and you're comfortable, let's get started.

In this chapter, I'll start by showing you how to modify master slides, handouts, and notes in PowerPoint. Next, I'll show you how to change presentation options and views so that your presentation will look the way you want.

After we finish creating a presentation, I'll show you how to configure the presentation to be printed in case you want to have your audience follow along with your presentation using a printed version. You'll also learn how to configure your presentation to get it ready to be presented to your audience.

Finally, I'll show you how to share your presentation with others so that they can provide their feedback and allow you to manage the review process.

I'll have an exercise at the end of every section in this chapter so that you can practice doing different tasks. Then, at the end of this chapter, you'll find a set of Review Questions that mimic the test questions you'll see on the MO-300 exam.

Modifying Slide Masters, Handout Masters, and Note Masters

You may be familiar with *styles* in Word, which are small files that contain formatting information that you can apply to selected text just by clicking on the style name. Though PowerPoint doesn't have styles, they use their equivalent: *masters*. That is, masters allow you to create one slide with information that you always use in a slide, such as your company logo and text with a specific font. You can also create more than one *slide master*, so when you create a new slide, you can quickly apply the appropriate master.

Microsoft realizes that you may also want to give your audience handouts of the presentation so that they can follow along and make notes of their own on the pages with each slide. PowerPoint allows you to make handout masters with information on each page of the handout, such as your company logo in the lower-right corner of each page.

PowerPoint wouldn't be a program worthy of the name presentation software if it didn't allow you to make notes that you can use to keep you on track during your presentation. You can also create note masters with a format that works best for you as you give your presentation.

Design Your Masters First

When you create a new presentation, it's a good idea to design all the masters first so that you can figure out what everything is going to look like. Once you set up your masters, you will find that slide creation goes more quickly. (It's a lot like preparing a wall properly before you start painting.)

If you edit any of the slide masters, PowerPoint does not make any changes to the affected slides with those masters. Instead, you need to reapply the new master to a slide. So, if you find that you need to make changes, do so early in the slide creation process. That way, you won't have to apply your master changes to very many slides and you save some time.

Changing the Slide Master Theme or Background

When you open a blank PowerPoint presentation, you see placeholders for adding a title and subtitle. You also see the Design Ideas panel on the right side of the PowerPoint window. When you want to change the slide master theme and/or background for your needs, you can create a new master in Slide Master view.

Open the Slide Master screen by clicking the View menu option, and then click Slide Master in the View menu ribbon (see Figure 1.1).

The Slide Master screen shows a variety of slide master templates on the right side of the PowerPoint window, the slide itself on the right side, and options in the Slide Master menu ribbon, as shown in Figure 1.2.

Within the Slide Master ribbon, you can change both the style theme as well as the background.

FIGURE 1.1   Slide Master option in the Master Views section

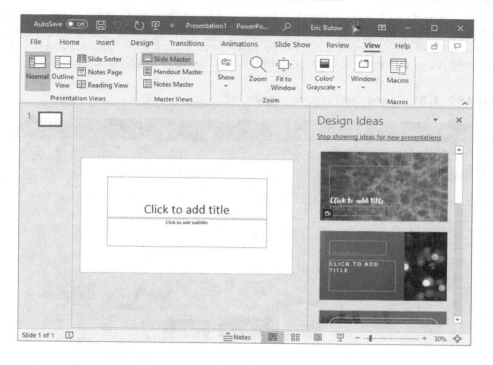

FIGURE 1.2   Slide Master screen

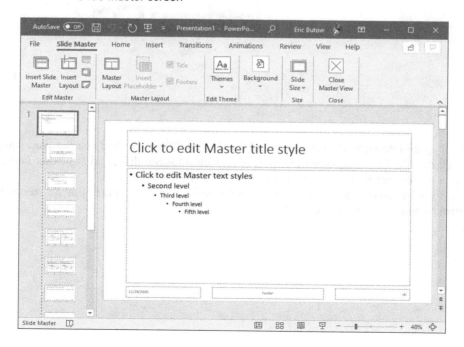

Apply a Slide Master theme

A slide master *theme* is a saved group of format and layout settings for your slides. Apply a slide master theme by clicking the Themes icon in the Edit Theme section in the Slide Master ribbon. A list of themes appears in the drop-down list, and each theme appears as a thumbnail-sized tile so that you can see what each tile looks like, as shown in Figure 1.3.

FIGURE 1.3 Theme tiles in the drop-down list

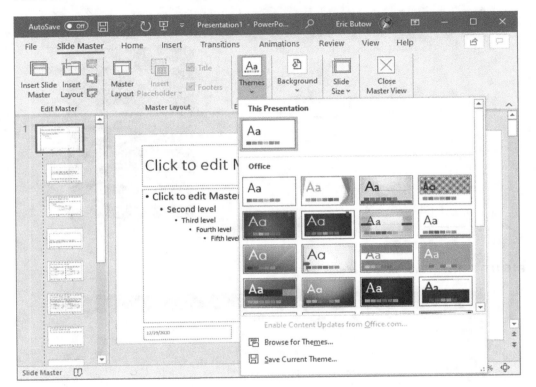

Scroll up and down in the list to view all the themes. When you find one that you want to use, click the tile. The slide shows the font, background for the slide, and any other features, such as a footer area that you can click to change the footer text.

When you're satisfied with the theme, click Close Master View in the Slide Master ribbon to return to editing an individual slide.

If you have an existing style theme that you use for your slideshows, such as one that your company requires you to use, you can open the theme by clicking Browse For Themes at the bottom of the drop-down list. Then you can browse to the appropriate folder and open the file, which will be added to the tiles within the Themes drop-down menu.

Change the Slide Master Background

If your master slide has a blank background or a background that's part of a theme, you can change just the background to one that's more to your liking. Start by opening the Slide Master menu ribbon, which you learned to do earlier in this chapter.

Next, change the background style by clicking Background Styles in the Background section in the Slide Master ribbon. A dozen tiles with different background types appear in the drop-down menu, as shown in Figure 1.4.

FIGURE 1.4   Background tiles in the drop-down list

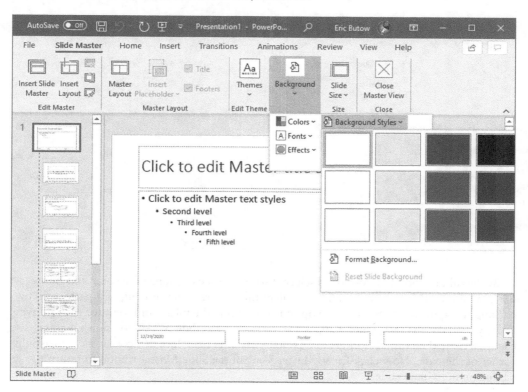

Move the mouse pointer over a tile to preview how the background will look in the slide. Click a tile to apply the background to the slide master.

If none of the background tiles meets your fancy, select Format Background at the bottom of the drop-down list. The Format Background pane appears at the right side of the Power-Point window (see Figure 1.5).

FIGURE 1.5   Format Background pane

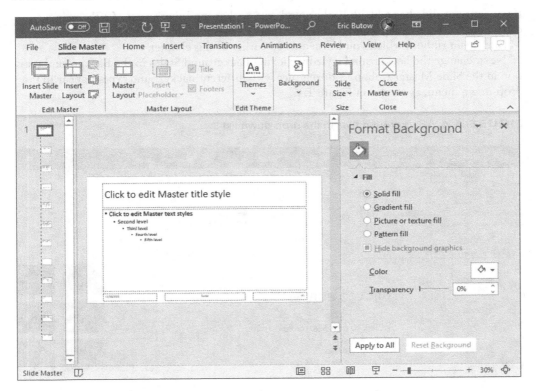

By default, the Solid Fill option is selected so that you can change the color and transparency of the fill. You can also add a gradient fill, picture or texture fill, or a pattern fill by clicking the appropriate button. The options for editing the fill are different for each fill type.

As you make changes, your changes appear within the slide. When you finish making changes, close the Format Background pane by clicking the Close (X) icon in the upper-right corner of the pane. Now click Close Master View in the Slide Master ribbon to return to editing an individual slide.

Modifying Slide Master Content

A new *slideshow* contains one master slide and 11 *layouts* within that master slide. These layouts have different formatting so that you can quickly apply one layout for a particular slide.

So why have a slide master? One good reason is that you can't apply a background to all layouts in a master—only the background in the selected layout. If you want to have the background apply to all layouts, and if you want to put the same features (like footers) in all layouts, then you must alter the slide master itself. Here's how to do that:

1. Click the View menu option.

2. In the Master Views section in the View ribbon, click the Slide Master icon.

3. In the Slide Master pane on the left side of the PowerPoint window, click the thumbnail-sized master slide at the very top of the pane. (You may need to scroll up to see it.)

4. Click the Slide Master menu option.

5. In the Master Layout section in the Slide Master ribbon, click Master Layout, as shown in Figure 1.6.

FIGURE 1.6   Master Layout icon in the ribbon

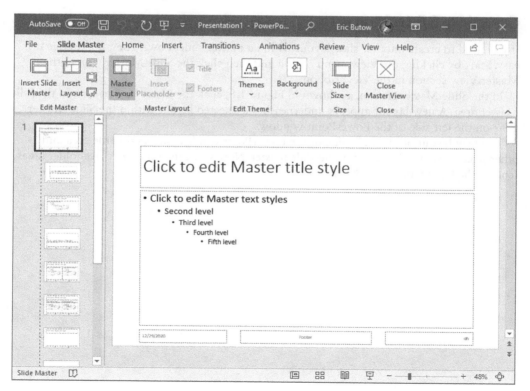

6. In the Master Layout dialog box, shown in Figure 1.7, select one of the check boxes to hide the feature in the master slide and all of the layouts.

7. When you're done, click OK.

FIGURE 1.7 Master Layout dialog box

The features that you decided to hide no longer appear in the slide master or in the layouts. When you want to return to editing individual slides, click the Close Master View icon in the View ribbon.

Creating Slide Layouts

If you need to create another slide layout within a master slide, PowerPoint makes this task easy. Start by clicking the View menu option and then click the Slide Master icon in the Master View section in the View ribbon.

In the Slide Master ribbon, as shown in Figure 1.8, click the Insert Layout icon in the Edit Master area. A new layout appears underneath the selected layout within the Slide Master pane on the left side of the PowerPoint window.

The new layout on the right side of the PowerPoint window shows the title area and other page elements contained in the slide master. Now you can add more placeholder areas, rename the layout, or delete the layout.

FIGURE 1.8   Insert Layout icon

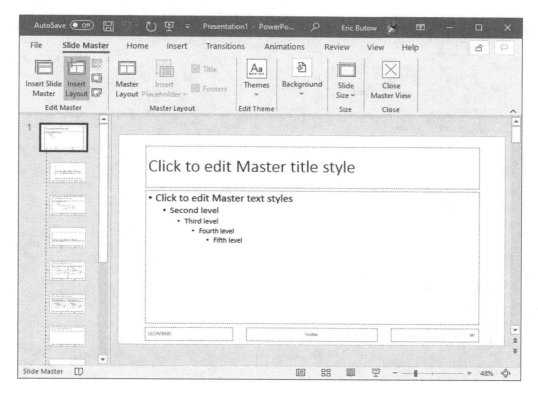

Add Placeholder Areas

You can add more *placeholder areas* for text and graphics that you can then edit either within the layout or within an individual slide that has the layout applied to it. Here's how to add a placeholder area in a layout:

1. Click Insert Placeholder in the Master Layout section in the Slide Master ribbon.

2. Select one of the eight content type options from the drop-down menu (see Figure 1.9).

FIGURE 1.9 Eight content type options in the drop-down menu

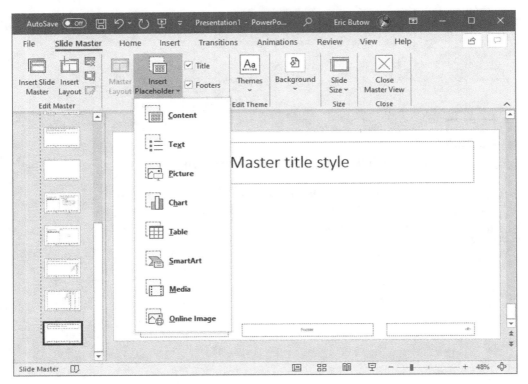

3. Move the cursor over the layout slide. When you do, the cursor changes to a cross.

4. Click, hold, and drag across the area where you want to draw the placeholder area.

5. Release the mouse button.

The information that appears in the placeholder area depends on the content type that you selected in step 2. For example, if you selected Content from the drop-down menu, then you see sample text in five different levels of a bulleted list.

You can resize a placeholder within the slide by clicking and holding on one of the sizing handles around the edge of the placeholder, and then dragging the placeholder to the size that you want. If you want to resize both the vertical and horizontal dimensions of the placeholder, click and hold on one of the corner sizing handles.

You can also move a placeholder area by clicking and holding within the placeholder area and then dragging to a new location in the slide. The cursor changes to a four-headed arrow when you move the mouse pointer over the area and when you drag it. PowerPoint also snaps the placeholder to specific points on the slide grid so that your content will be aligned properly in the layout.

Rename the Layout

You can give a new layout its own unique name so that you can find it easily when you apply the layout to a slide. Change the layout name by clicking Rename in the Edit Master section in the Slide Master ribbon. (If the width of your PowerPoint window is limited, click the Rename icon in the Edit Master section.) The Rename Layout dialog box has the default name selected within the Layout Name box (see Figure 1.10).

FIGURE 1.10   Rename Layout dialog box

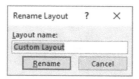

Press the Backspace key, type the new name, and then click Rename. PowerPoint makes no visible changes, but when you apply the layout to an individual slide, you will see the new layout name in the list. You will learn more about applying a layout to a slide in Chapter 2, "Managing Slides."

Delete the Layout

If you want to delete a layout, you have two ways to do it:

- Click on the layout in the Slide Master pane on the left side of the PowerPoint window. Then press Delete on your keyboard.

- Click on the layout in the Slide Master pane, and then click Delete in the Edit Master area in the Slide Master ribbon, as shown in Figure 1.11. (If the width of your PowerPoint window is limited, click the Delete icon in the Edit Master section.)

FIGURE 1.11 Delete icon in Slide Master ribbon

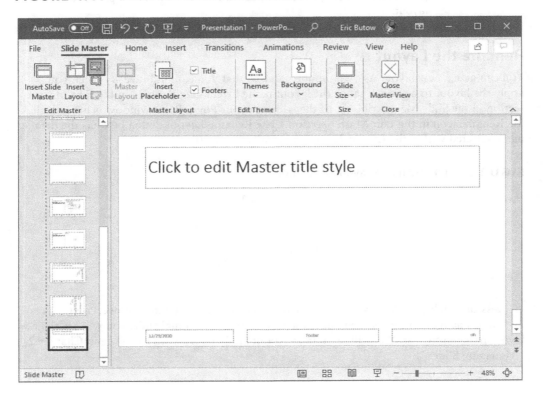

In both cases, PowerPoint deletes the layout and displays the layout directly underneath the deleted layout in the list.

Modify Slide Layouts

You can modify slide layouts using many of the tools that were already discussed in this chapter, including adding a placeholder, changing the theme, and changing the background. The Slide Master ribbon also contains several other options for changing layout features.

Title and Footers Check Boxes   In the Master Layout section, select the Title and/or Footers check boxes, as shown in Figure 1.12, to hide the title section and/or the footers section in a layout, respectively. You can clear the check boxes to display the title and/or footer in the layout.

FIGURE 1.12   Title and Footers check boxes

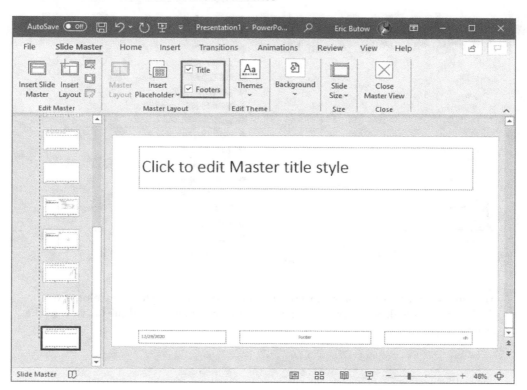

Colors   Click Colors in the Background area to open the drop-down list of color schemes that you can apply to a layout (see Figure 1.13). Scroll up and down in the list to view all the schemes and click a scheme to apply it to the layout. As you move the mouse pointer over the color scheme, the scheme appears in the layout so that you can preview how the colors look before you commit to the scheme.

FIGURE 1.13   Color scheme drop-down list

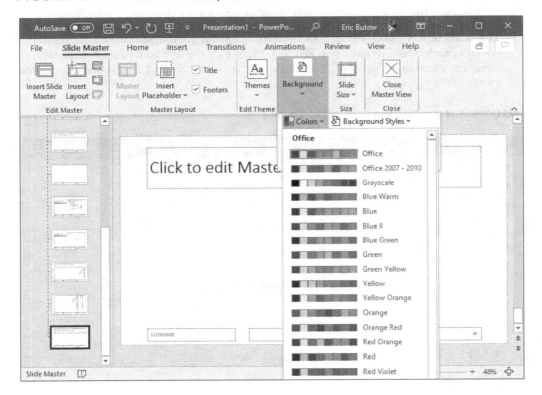

You can also set custom colors for your layout by selecting Customize Colors from the bottom of the drop-down list, but customizing colors is beyond the purview of the exam.

Fonts   Click Fonts in the Background area to show the drop-down list of font schemes that you can apply to a layout, as shown in Figure 1.14. The scheme is listed with the title font above the font for the rest of the text in the layout.

FIGURE 1.14   Font scheme drop-down list

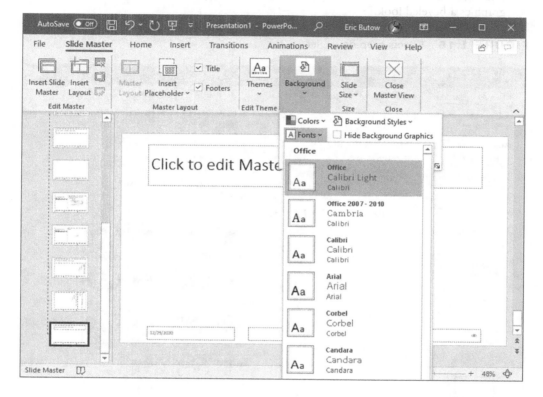

Scroll up and down in the list to view all the schemes and click a scheme to apply it to the layout. As you move the mouse pointer over the font scheme, the scheme appears in the layout so that you can preview how the fonts look before you commit to the scheme.

You can also set custom fonts for your layout by selecting Customize Fonts from the bottom of the drop-down list, but customizing fonts is not covered on the MO-300 exam.

Effects   Click Effects in the Background area to show a drop-down list of effects (see Figure 1.15) that you can apply to graphics in a layout, such as Inset to give your graphics a beveled look.

FIGURE 1.15   Effects drop-down list

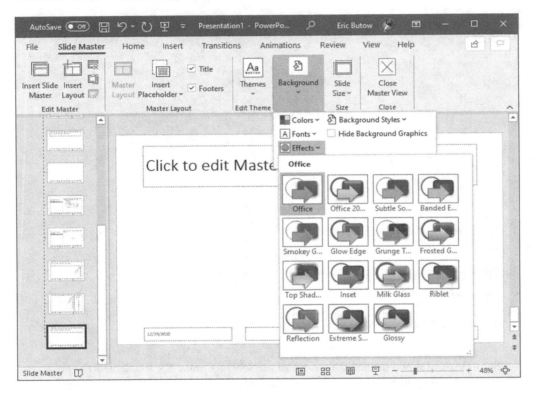

If you have any graphics in the layout, then as you move the mouse pointer over the effect, PowerPoint applies the effect to the graphic so that you can preview how the graphic looks in the layout before you apply the effect.

Hide Background Graphics   If you don't want to show graphics in the background of your layout and any slides that have the layout applied, select the Hide Background Graphics check box, as shown in Figure 1.16. If you decide that you want to show the background graphic(s) at any point in the future, clear the check box.

FIGURE 1.16   Hide Background Graphics check box

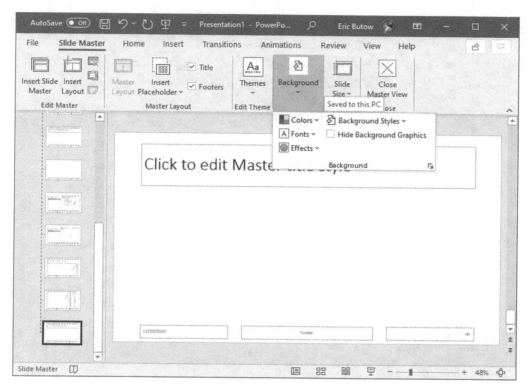

Modifying the Handout Master

The layout requirements for slides, handouts, and notes are different, so it's no surprise that PowerPoint has separate functions for changing masters for all three categories. The Handout Master screen allows you to edit how your handouts look, including the layout, headers, footers, and the background.

 When you make changes to a handout master, the changes appear on all pages of the handout when you print it to paper or to a PDF file.

Modify the Handout Master by clicking the View menu option and then clicking Handout Master in the Master Views section in the View ribbon, as shown in Figure 1.17.

FIGURE 1.17   The Handout Master option

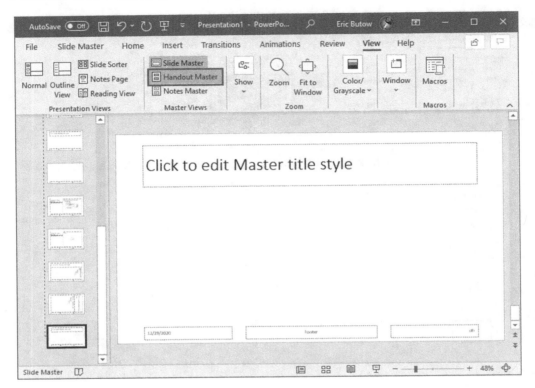

The Handout Master menu ribbon opens by default (see Figure 1.18), so you can select one of the following options in the ribbon:

Handout Orientation   Select the orientation of handout pages: Portrait (8.5 inches wide by 11 inches high) and Landscape (11 inches wide by 8.5 inches high). The default orientation is Portrait.

Slide Size   Change the size of each slide on handout pages between Widescreen (a 16:9 aspect ratio) or Standard (a 4:3 aspect ratio). The default size is Widescreen. You can also set a custom screen size, which you will learn about later in this chapter.

Slides Per Page   Choose how many slides you want to place on each handout page. The default is 6 slides, as shown in Figure 1.19. However, you can also choose between 1, 2, 3, 4, and 9 slides on a page. You can also display only the slideshow outline without any slides.

FIGURE 1.18   Handout Master ribbon

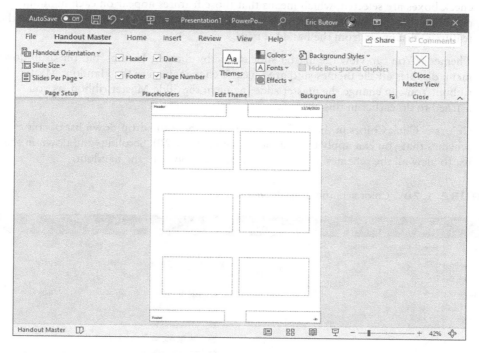

FIGURE 1.19   Slides Per Page drop-down list

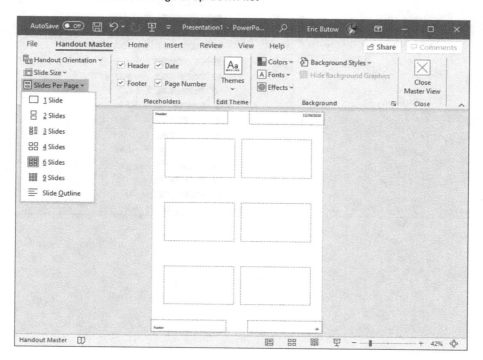

Placeholders   In the Placeholders section, the Header, Footer, Date, and Page Number check boxes are selected, which means that those features appear on each handout page. Select one or more of the check boxes to hide those features on the page, and the feature(s) disappear from the handout page.

Themes   You can view the master slide theme by clicking Themes, but the drop-down menu disables all the themes so that you can't change them in the Handout Master ribbon. You can change the master slide theme in the Slide Master ribbon, as you learned to do earlier in this chapter.

Colors   Click Colors in the Background area to show the drop-down list of color schemes that you can apply to a handout (see Figure 1.20). Scroll up and down in the list to view all the schemes and click a scheme to apply it to the handout.

FIGURE 1.20   Color scheme drop-down list

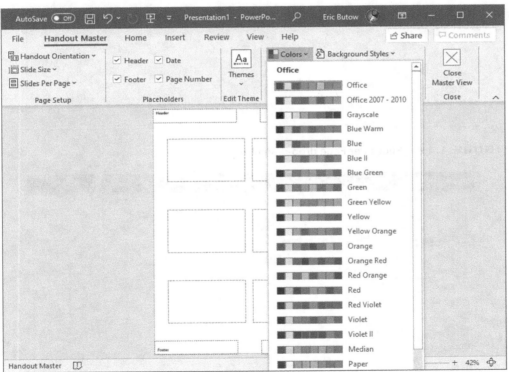

You can also set custom colors for your layout by selecting Customize Colors from the bottom of the drop-down list, but customizing colors is not covered on the MO-300 exam.

Fonts   Click Fonts to show the drop-down list of font schemes that you can apply to a layout, as shown in Figure 1.21. The scheme is listed with the title font above the font for the rest of the text in the layout.

FIGURE 1.21   Font schemes in the drop-down list

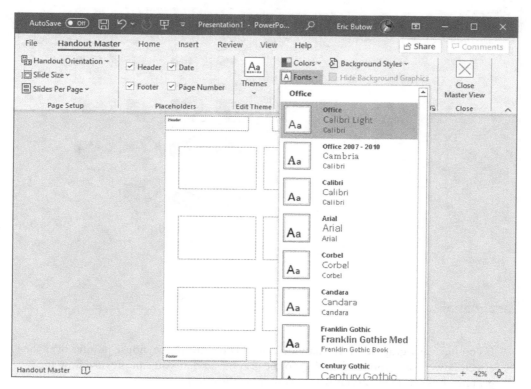

Scroll up and down in the list to view all the schemes and click a scheme to apply it to the layout. When you click the scheme, the fonts change on the page.

You can also set custom fonts for your layout by selecting Customize Fonts from the bottom of the drop-down list, but customizing fonts is not covered on the MO-300 exam.

Effects Click Effects to show a drop-down list of effects (see Figure 1.22) that you can apply to graphics in a handout.

FIGURE 1.22 Effects drop-down list

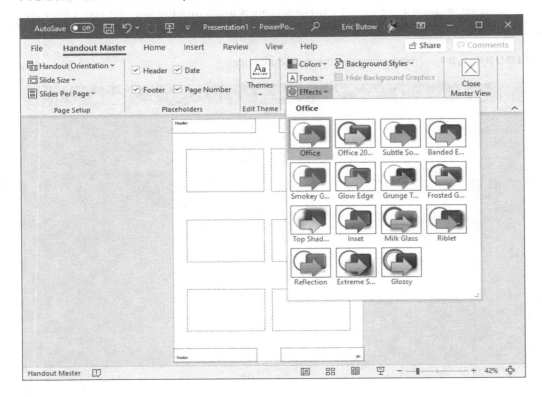

If you have any graphics in the handout, then as you move the mouse pointer over the effect, PowerPoint applies the effect to the graphic so that you can preview how the graphic looks in the handout before you apply the effect.

Background Change the background style in the handout by clicking Background Styles. A dozen tiles with different background types appears in the drop-down menu, as shown in Figure 1.23.

FIGURE 1.23 Background tiles in the drop-down list

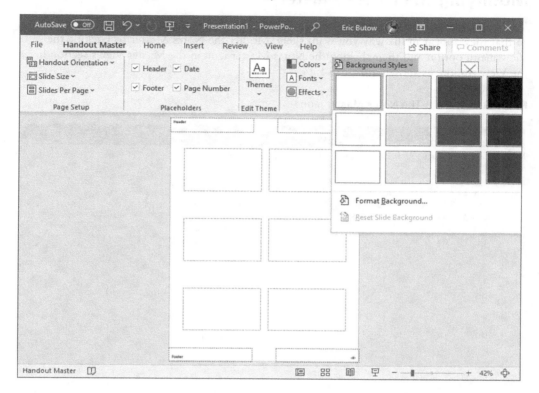

Move the mouse pointer over a tile to preview how the background will look in the slide. Click a tile to apply the background to the Handout Master.

If none of the background tiles meets your fancy, select Format Background from the bottom of the drop-down list. Formatting Handout Master backgrounds is beyond the scope of the exam.

Hide Background Graphics   If you don't want to show graphics in the background of your layout and any slides that have the layout applied, select the Hide Background Graphics check box. If you decide that you want to show the background graphic(s) at any point in the future, clear the check box.

Close Master View   Click the Close Master View icon to stop editing the Handout Master and to return to editing individual slides.

Modifying the Notes Master

When you want to refer to notes as you give your presentation, you can format your notes so that they appear in the way you want them. Modify the Notes Master by clicking the View menu option and then clicking the Notes Master icon in the Master Views section in the View ribbon, as shown in Figure 1.24.

FIGURE 1.24   The Notes Master icon

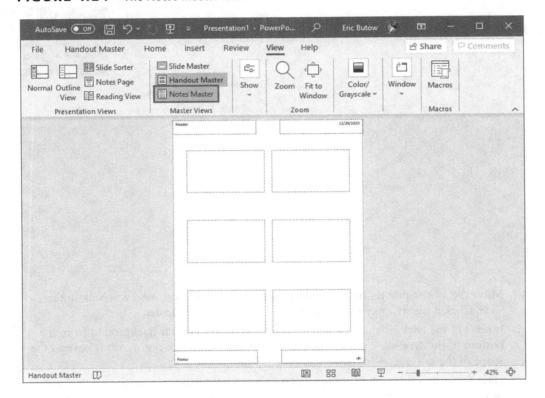

The Notes Master menu ribbon opens by default (see Figure 1.25) so that you can select one of the following options in the ribbon.

FIGURE 1.25   Notes Master ribbon

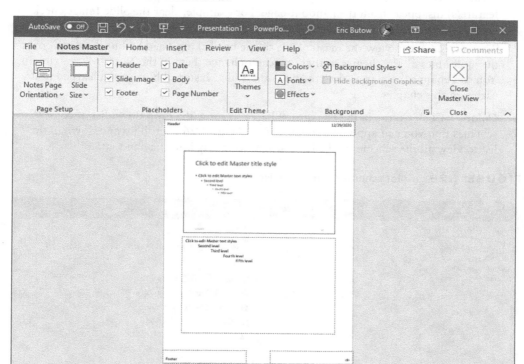

Notes Page Orientation   Select the orientation of notes pages: Portrait (8.5 inches wide by 11 inches high) or Landscape (11 inches wide by 8.5 inches high). The default orientation is Portrait.

Slide Size   Change the size of each slide on handout pages between Widescreen (a 16:9 aspect ratio) or Standard (a 4:3 aspect ratio). The default size is Widescreen. You can also set a custom screen size, which you will learn about later in this chapter.

Placeholders   In the Placeholders section, the Header, Slide Image, Footer, Date, Body, and Page Number check boxes are selected, which means that those features appear on each handout page.

Clear one or more of the check boxes to hide those features on the page, and the feature(s) disappear from the handout page. For example, clear the Slide Image check box to hide slides from each notes page.

Themes   You can view the master slide theme by clicking Themes, but the drop-down menu disables all the themes so that you can't change them in the Notes Master ribbon. You can change the master slide theme in the Slide Master ribbon as you learned to do earlier in this chapter.

Colors   Click Colors in the Background area to show the drop-down list of color schemes that you can apply to a handout (see Figure 1.26). Scroll up and down in the list to view all the schemes and click a scheme to apply it to the handout.

FIGURE 1.26   Color scheme drop-down list

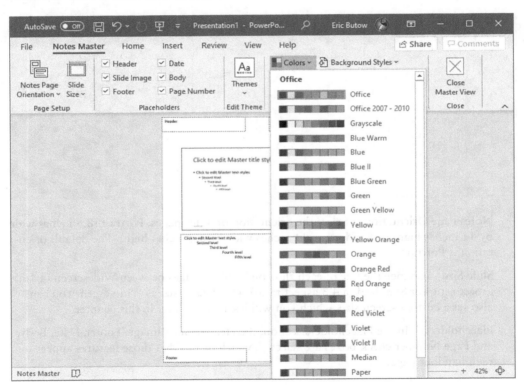

You can also set custom colors for your layout by selecting Customize Colors from the bottom of the drop-down list, but customizing colors is not included on the MO-300 exam.

Fonts   Click Fonts to show the drop-down list of font schemes that you can apply to a layout, as shown in Figure 1.27. The scheme is listed with the title font above the font for the rest of the text in the layout.

FIGURE 1.27   Font schemes in the drop-down list

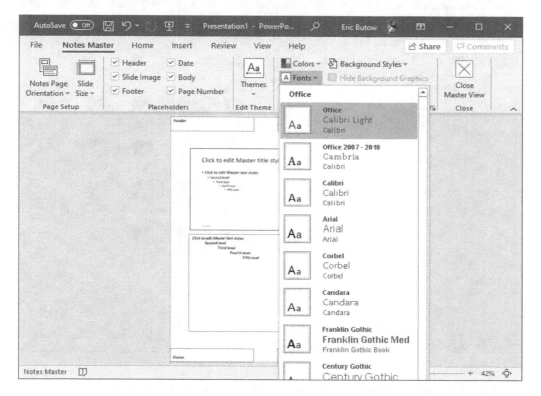

Scroll up and down in the list to view all the schemes and click a scheme to apply it to the layout. When you click the scheme, the fonts change on the page.

You can also set custom fonts for your layout by selecting Customize Fonts from the bottom of the drop-down list, but customizing fonts is beyond the purview of the exam.

Effects   Click Effects to show a drop-down list of effects (see Figure 1.28) that you can apply to graphics in a handout.

FIGURE 1.28   Effects drop-down list

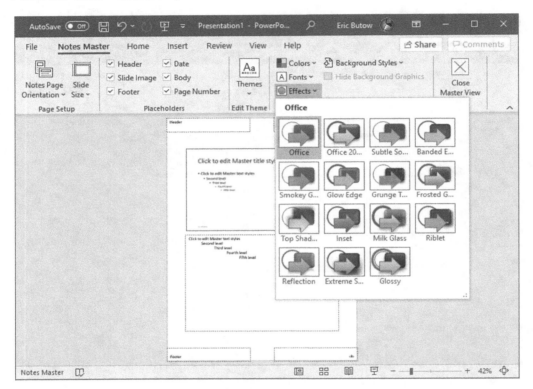

If you have any graphics in the handout, then as you move the mouse pointer over the effect, PowerPoint applies the effect to the graphic so that you can preview how the graphic looks in the handout before you apply the effect.

Background   Change the background style in the handout by clicking Background Styles. A dozen tiles with different background types appear in the drop-down menu, as shown in Figure 1.29.

FIGURE 1.29   Background tiles in the drop-down list

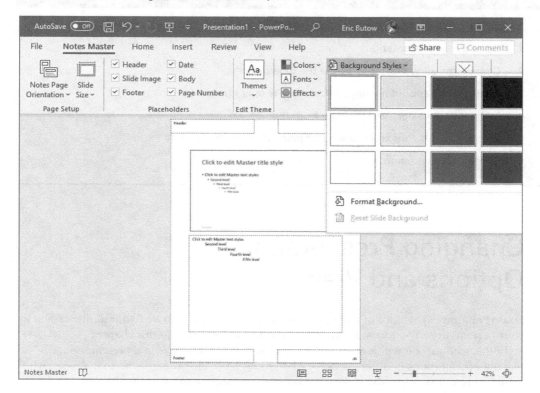

Move the mouse pointer over a tile to preview how the background will look in the slide. Click a tile to apply the background to the handout master.

If none of the background tiles meets your fancy, select Format Background from the bottom of the drop-down list. Formatting handout master backgrounds is not covered on the MO-300 exam.

Hide Background Graphics   If you don't want to show graphics in the background of your layout and any slides that have the layout applied, select the Hide Background Graphics check box. If you decide that you want to show the background graphic(s) at any point in the future, clear the check box.

Close Master View   Click the Close Master View icon to stop editing the handout master and return to editing individual slides.

EXERCISE 1.1

Modifying Slide Masters, Handout Masters, and Note Masters

1. Open a new presentation.

2. Change the slide master to one of the blue themes.

3. Change the handout master so that there is only one slide per page.

4. In the notes master, hide the date from the notes pages.

5. Create a new layout and place a text placeholder in the layout.

6. Save the presentation.

Changing Presentation Options and Views

PowerPoint gives you a lot of power to change what you see and what your audience sees in your presentation. You learned a little about some of this earlier in this chapter.

In this section, you will learn more about changing the slide size in a presentation, displaying presentations in different views, and setting basic file properties so that anyone who wants more information about the creation of the slideshow can view it.

Changing the Slide Size

When you don't want to go through the trouble of having to change the screen size for your presentation within the slide master, you can change the size of all the slides when you edit individual slides. Here's how to do this:

1. Click the Design menu option.

2. In the Customize section in the Design ribbon, click Slide Size. (If the width of your PowerPoint window is limited, click the Customize icon and then click Style Size.)

3. Select Standard (4:3) or Widescreen (16:9) from the drop-down list, as shown in Figure 1.30.

FIGURE 1.30 Slide Size drop-down list

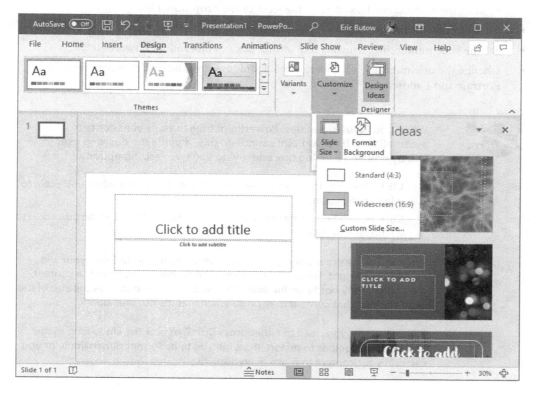

FIGURE 1.31 Slide Size dialog box

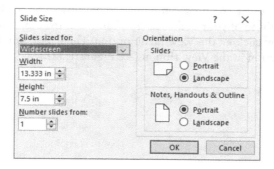

You can also customize the slide size by clicking Custom Slide Size at the bottom of the menu. The Slide Size dialog box, shown in Figure 1.31, allows you to do the following:

- Select a preexisting size from the Slides Sized For area. Just click the down arrow to the right of the Widescreen box to view the sizes in the drop-down list.
- Set a custom width and height.
- Set the slide numbering, which is like setting page numbering in PowerPoint.
- Change the orientation of all slides, notes, handouts, and the outline pages between Portrait and Landscape.

When you resize the slides, PowerPoint tries to scale your content automatically. If PowerPoint cannot do this, it punts the decision over to you by opening a dialog box and giving you two resizing options:

- Click Maximize to increase the size of the slide content when you scale to a larger slide size.
- Click Ensure Fit to decrease the size of the slide content when you scale to a smaller slide size.

After you make the changes, you should check to make sure that your slide content looks right. For example, when you increase the size of the content, the content may not fit on the slide. Conversely, if you decrease the size of the slide content, that content may be so small that it's not readable.

In those cases, you need to either press Ctrl+Z or click the Undo icon in the Quick Access Toolbar to restore the slide size to its former dimensions, or you can edit your content to make everything fit.

Displaying Presentations in Different Views

As with any other Microsoft 365 program, PowerPoint allows you to change views to match your needs as well as those of your audience. You can select from one of five different views that you can display by clicking the View menu option. The five option icons appear in the Presentation Views section in the View ribbon (see Figure 1.32).

FIGURE 1.32   Icons in the Presentation Views section

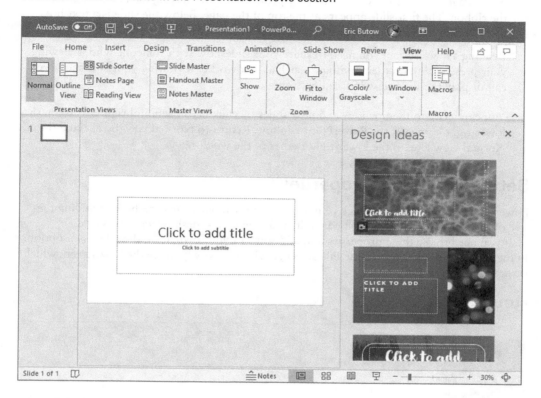

By default, PowerPoint selects Normal view, which shows you the list of slides in the pane on the left and the current slide you're editing in the pane on the right. You can change your view by clicking one of the following four icons:

Outline View   Shows the outline text in the left pane in outline form so that you can begin typing your text. When you finish typing the first entry in your outline, press Enter to continue to the next line. Each line in the outline is a new slide.

Press Tab to create a bulleted, indented entry below the main level (or Level 1) entry. This new bulleted entry is also the first bullet in the associated slide.

Slide Sorter   The Slide Sorter view shows thumbnail images of your slides so that you can review them quickly. You can reorder the slides by clicking and holding on a slide and then dragging to a new location within the window. As you move the slide, other slides move aside to make room for your moved slide. Double-click a slide to edit it in Outline view.

Notes Page Add notes quickly to your presentation by clicking the Notes Page icon in the ribbon. The first slide appears at the top of the page. Below the slide is a text box. Click within the text box to start typing notes associated with the slide.

Reading View When you need to share your slideshow with someone who is viewing your presentation on their computer, such as a coworker reviewing your slideshow, you can display the slideshow in Reading view.

You can move to the previous and next slides by clicking the left and right arrows in the lower-right corner of the PowerPoint window. Return to Normal view by clicking the Normal view icon in the lower-right corner of the window.

Setting Basic File Properties

PowerPoint constantly keeps track of basic properties about your slideshow, including the size of the slideshow file, who last edited it, and when the slideshow was last saved.

If you need to see these properties and add some of your own, click the File menu option. In the menu on the left side of the File screen, click Info. Now you see the Info screen, which is shown in Figure 1.33.

FIGURE 1.33 Info screen

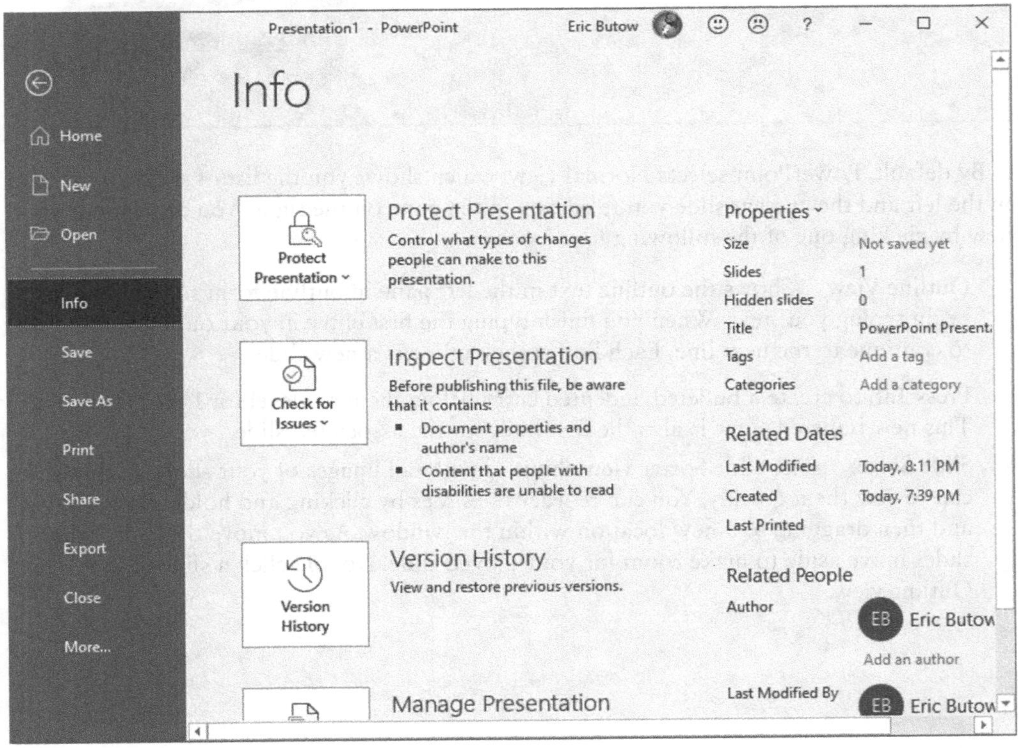

The Properties section appears at the right side of the screen. Scroll up and down in the Info screen to view more properties. PowerPoint doesn't show all properties by default, but you can reveal the hidden properties by clicking the Show All Properties link at the bottom of the Properties section.

You can also add properties, including a slideshow title, a tag (which is the Microsoft term for a keyword), and a category. For example, click Add A Tag in the Properties section and type one or more tags in the box.

EXERCISE 1.2

Changing Presentation Options and Views

1. Open a new presentation.

2. Change the slide size to Standard.

3. Add three slides with text information in Outline view.

4. View your slideshow in Reading view.

5. Return to Normal view and save your presentation.

Configuring Print Settings for Presentations

You may want to print your slideshow to look at it on paper (or have people comment on the printed copies tacked to a wall). Printing handouts is also a common task in PowerPoint; for example, you can copy a master and distribute the copies to your attendees. If you prefer not to use a second computer or to have your screen split, you may want to print your notes as well.

PowerPoint has you covered. You can print all slides or some of the slides within a slideshow, print some or all notes pages, and decide if you want to print in color or monochrome (if you have a color printer, that is).

Printing All or Part of a Presentation

When you want to print some slides or all slides from your slideshow, follow these steps:

1. Click the File menu option.

2. On the File screen, click Print in the menu on the left side of the screen.

3. Click the Print All Slides button to view the print options in the drop-down menu, as shown in Figure 1.34.

FIGURE 1.34   Print options

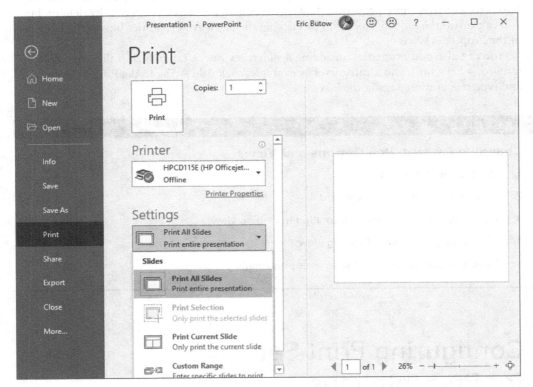

Now you can select from one of the following options to print your presentation in the Print screen:

Print All Slides: This is the default option that prints all slides in your slideshow.

Print Selection: After you click this option, the button changes to Print Selection. Now you can print one or more slides by typing the slide number(s) in the Slides box that appears directly underneath the Print Selection box.

Print Current Slide: After you click this option, the button changes to Print Current Slide. This means PowerPoint only prints the current slide shown in the print preview pane on the right side of the Print screen. The slide in the print preview pane shows its associated slide number.

Custom Range: After you click this option, the button changes to Custom Range. Type the slide number(s) that you want to print in the Slides box directly underneath the Custom Range box.

In the Slides box, indicate groups of slides by placing a hyphen between the slide numbers. For example, **4-6** means that you will print slides 4, 5, and 6 in your slideshow. Separate individual or groups of slides with commas, such as **1,3,5-9,11**. You do not need to add a space after each comma.

Printing Notes Pages

When you want to print one slide and all the notes for that slide on each printed page, here's what to do:

1. Click the File menu option.

2. On the File screen, click Print in the menu on the left side of the screen.

3. Click the Full Page Slides button to view the print layout options in the drop-down menu, as shown in Figure 1.35.

FIGURE 1.35   Print Layout options

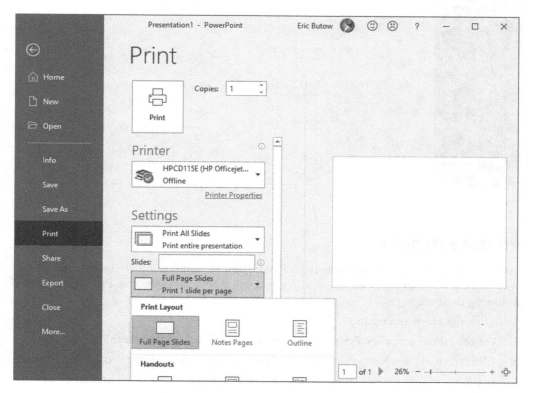

Select Notes Pages from the drop-down list. The button changes to Notes Pages, and the slide in the print preview area shows the slide at the top and the notes area at the bottom (see Figure 1.36).

FIGURE 1.36   Notes area below the slide on the page

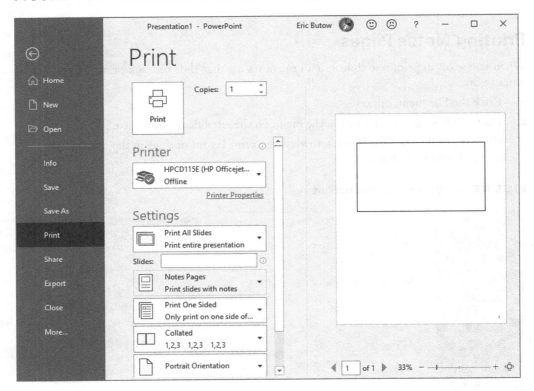

Printing Handouts

Perhaps the most common printouts from PowerPoint are handouts that you distribute to your audience so that they can follow along and make notes of their own. Print handouts by following these steps:

1. Click the File menu option.

2. On the File screen, click Print in the menu on the left side of the screen.

3. Click the Full Page Slides button to view print layout options in the drop-down menu.

4. In the Handouts section, shown in Figure 1.37, click one of the nine handout print option icons.

FIGURE 1.37   Handouts section icons

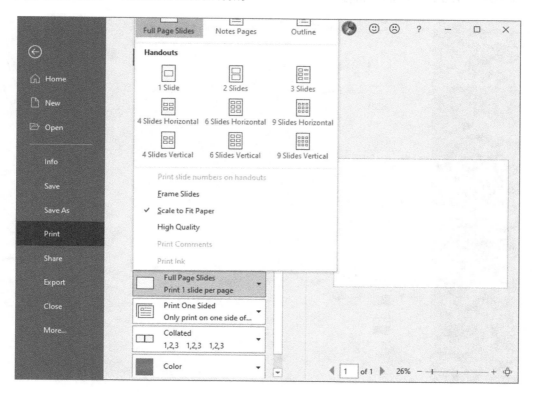

Each icon shows you how the slides will appear in the handout. Only the 3 Slides option has lines to the right of each slide so that people who receive the handout can write notes on those lines. The rest only show one to as many as nine slides on one page.

Printing in Color, Grayscale, or Black and White

If you have a color printer, you have the option of printing your presentation in full and vibrant color. You can also print in grayscale, which approximates colors into various shades of gray, or you can print in black and white. That is, any colors automatically print with black ink—even text to which you applied the gray color.

Choose your print color style by opening the Print screen as you learned to do earlier in this chapter. Now click the Color button in the Settings section. The drop-down menu with your color options appears, as shown in Figure 1.38.

The default setting is color, but when you click Grayscale or Pure Black and White, the slide in the print preview area changes to show you what the slide will look like with the setting applied.

FIGURE 1.38   Color settings list

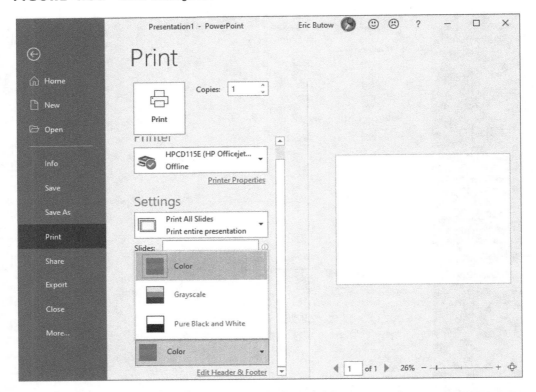

EXERCISE 1.3

Configuring Print Settings for Presentations

1.   Open a new slideshow.

2.   Create three slides and add text in each slide.

3.   Select slides 1 and 3 for printing.

4.   Print the handouts with note lines next to each slide.

5.   Print the slides.

6.   Save the slideshow by pressing Ctrl+S.

Configuring and Presenting Slideshows

When you're ready to present your slideshow, PowerPoint gives you several options to customize slideshows for your audience. You can also rehearse your slideshow *timing* so that each new slide appears in time with recorded audio, and you can set up recording options. Once you're done, you can present your slideshow in Presenter View.

Creating Custom Slideshows

You can show a certain number of slides of a slideshow for a specific audience only. For example, you may want to show the slides with financial charts in a presentation to the sales team. PowerPoint creates a custom show so that you can place specific slides in your slideshow within the custom show.

You can create two types of custom slideshows. The first is a simple custom slideshow that appears on your computer, and the other is a custom slideshow that contains a hyperlink to a group of slides. The latter is useful if you have slides that you want to show to all employees and then have specific links for specific company departments.

Once you set up your custom slideshow, you can present it to your audience, either on your computer or from another website such as a company intranet.

Create a Simple Custom Slideshow

When you want to create a custom slideshow that you are going to bring with you on a laptop to share in a live presentation, follow these steps:

1. Click the Slide Show menu option.
2. In the Start Slide Show section in the Slide Show ribbon, click Custom Slide Show (see Figure 1.39).
3. Select Custom Shows from the drop-down menu.
4. In the Custom Shows dialog box, click New.
5. In the Define Custom Show dialog box, shown in Figure 1.40, press Backspace and then type the new slideshow name in the Slide Show Name box.
6. In the Slides In Presentation box, select the check boxes to the left of the names of slides that you want to add.
7. Click the Add button. The slides appear in the Slides In Custom Show list.
8. Click OK. The dialog box closes, and the custom show appears in the Custom Shows dialog box.
9. Click Close.

FIGURE 1.39 Custom Slide Show option in the ribbon

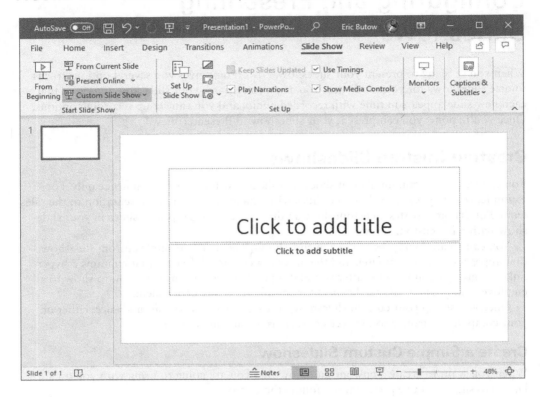

FIGURE 1.40 Define Custom Show dialog box

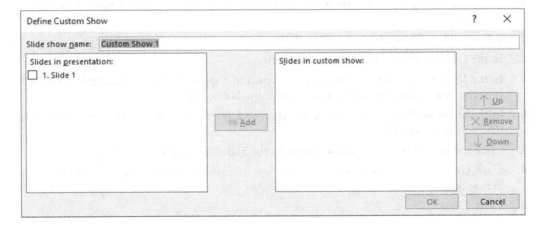

Create a Hyperlinked Custom Slideshow

After you create a custom slideshow for a specific audience, you can link text from one slide to those custom slides. Here's how to do that:

1. Go to the slide in your slideshow into which you want to place the link.
2. Click the Insert menu option.
3. In the Links section in the Insert ribbon, click Link (see Figure 1.41). (If the width of your PowerPoint window is limited, click the Links icon and then click Link.)

FIGURE 1.41 The Link option in the drop-down menu

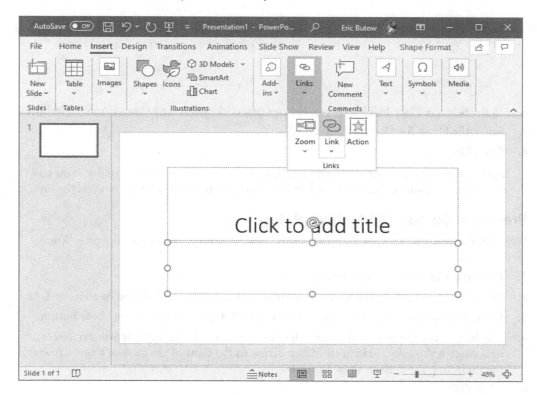

4. Select Insert Link from the drop-down menu.
5. In the Insert Hyperlink dialog box, as shown in Figure 1.42, click the Place In This Document icon.

FIGURE 1.42   The Place In This Document icon in the Link To section

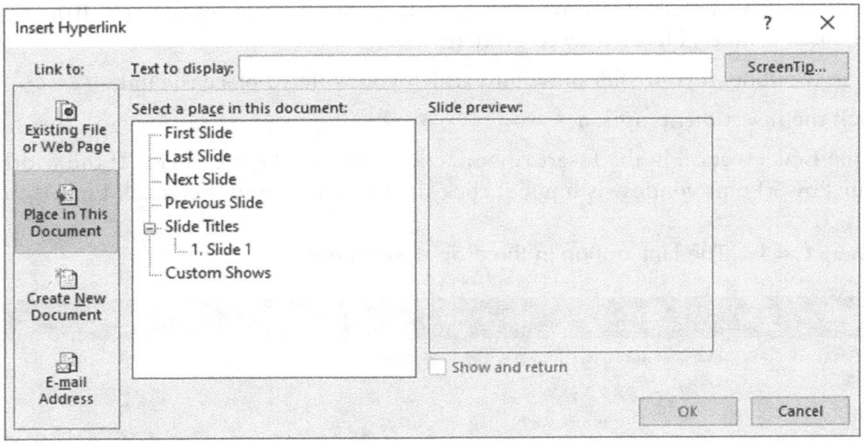

6.   In the Select A Place In This Document tree list, click the name of the custom slideshow.

7.   Select the Show And Return check box.

8.   Click OK.

When you run the presentation and you click the link in the slide, PowerPoint shows all the slides in your custom slideshow and then returns you to the slide that contains the link.

Present a Custom Slideshow Setup

When you're ready to set up your custom slideshow to present to your audience, follow these steps:

1.   Click the Slide Show menu option.

2.   In the Set Up section in the Slide Show ribbon, click Set Up Slide Show (see Figure 1.43).

3.   In the Set Up Show dialog box, shown in Figure 1.44, click the Custom Show button.

4.   The box below the button shows the first custom show in the list, but you can select a new custom show by clicking the down arrow to the right of the custom show name and then selecting the custom show in the list.

5.   Click OK.

FIGURE 1.43   Set Up Slide Show option in the ribbon

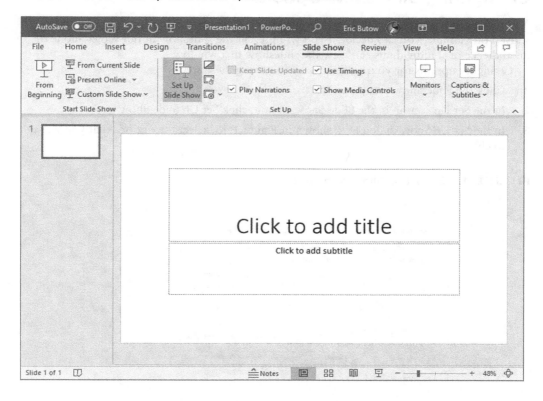

FIGURE 1.44   Custom Show button

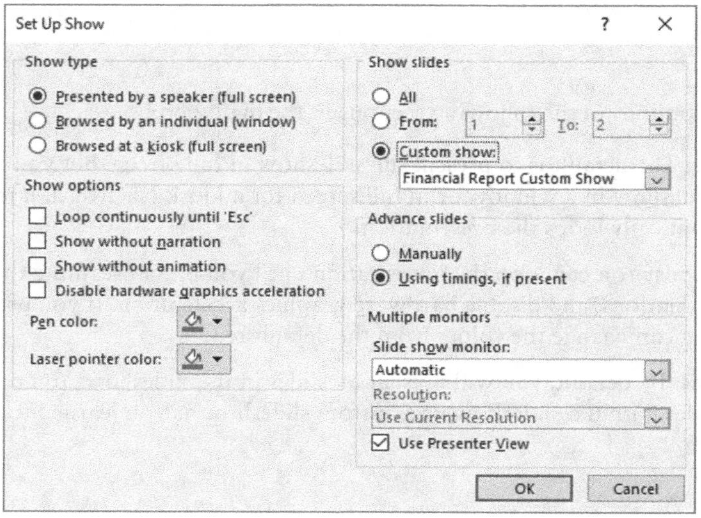

Configuring Slideshow Options

You may need to configure other slideshow options aside from preparing a custom slideshow. For example, you can decide if you will present the slideshow in full-screen mode to an audience or if individuals can view the slideshow in a window.

Configure options for your slideshow by following these steps:

1. Click the Slide Show menu option.

2. In the Set Up section in the Slide Show ribbon, click Set Up Slide Show.

3. In the Set Up Show dialog box, shown in Figure 1.45, select the options that you want to change.

FIGURE 1.45   Set Up Show dialog box

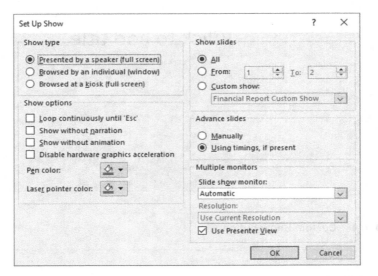

You can set options in the following sections in the dialog box:

Show Type: The default is to present the slideshow in full screen, but you can also present the slideshow in a window or in full screen for a kiosk (such as at a trade show) that automatically loops the presentation.

Show Options: You can loop the presentation until you press Esc, mute the narration, hide all animations, and disable hardware graphics acceleration. If you use a pen or laser pointer, you can change the colors from the default red.

Show Slides: By default, you will present all slides in the slideshow. You can show only specific slides within a slideshow or a custom slideshow as you learned to do earlier in this chapter.

Advance Slides: PowerPoint advances slides using timings if you have set them. You will learn how to change slide timing in the next section. You can also advance slides manually.

Multiple Monitors: You automatically present your slideshow on the default monitor. However, if your computer is connected to another device, such as a large TV or a projection system, you can change the default monitor and the video resolution. You can also present the slideshow in Presenter View, which you will learn about later in this chapter.

Rehearsing Slideshow Timing

When you record audio narration, or you feel confident that when you talk in a live presentation your slides will move in time with you, PowerPoint allows you to set the timing for your slides to move from one to the other.

Once you set the timing for each slide, PowerPoint makes it easy for you to rehearse and tweak your timing to match your audio narration or where you think you'll stop talking about one slide and you'll be ready to move to the next one.

Rehearse Your Timings

You can rehearse your slideshow timings by clicking the Slide Show menu option and then clicking the Rehearse Timings icon in the Set Up section in the Slide Show ribbon (see Figure 1.46). (If the width of your PowerPoint window is limited, click the Delete icon in the Edit Master section.)

The recording dialog box appears in the upper-left corner of the PowerPoint window and starts the clock, as shown in Figure 1.47, so you can start timing your first slide.

In the Recording dialog box, the recording time for the current slide is shown in the white box. The total recording time for the entire presentation is at the right side of the dialog box.

If you want to pause the recording, click the Pause icon to the left of the current time. When you're ready to resume, click Resume Recording in the PowerPoint dialog box in the center of the screen.

You can start the recording back at the beginning by clicking the Repeat icon immediately to the right of the recording time for the current slide. PowerPoint pauses the recording immediately so that you can get ready, and then you can click Resume Recording in the PowerPoint dialog box in the center of the screen.

When you're done, click the Next icon (it's a right arrow) to start recording the next slide.

After you finish rehearsing your timings, click the Close icon in the upper-right corner of the dialog box. A new dialog box appears in the center of the screen that tells you the length of the recording and asks if you want to save the slide timings. Click Yes to save the timings to the slideshow or No to reject them.

You can also stop recording by pressing the Esc key instead of clicking the Close icon.

FIGURE 1.46   Rehearse Timings icon in the ribbon

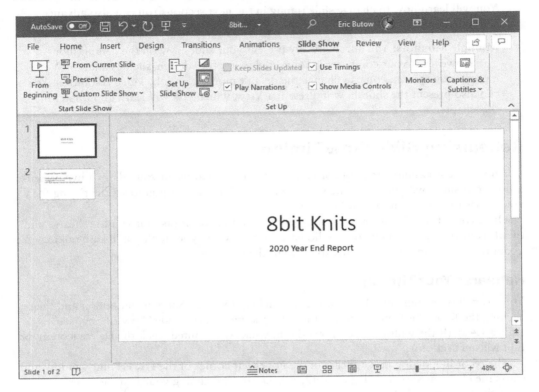

FIGURE 1.47   Recording dialog box

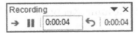

View and Turn Off Slideshow Timings

When you need to view your slideshow timings, click the View menu option and then click the Slide Sorter icon in the Presentation View section in the View ribbon. The recording time appears below the thumbnail image for each slide, as shown in Figure 1.48.

But what happens if you change your mind, or the presentation isn't going as you expected and you have to turn the timings off? There are two ways to do that.

Change the Timing Setup

Click the Slide Show menu option, and then click the Slide Show icon in the Set Up section in the Slide Show ribbon. In the Set Up Show dialog box, click the Manually button and then click OK (see Figure 1.49).

FIGURE 1.48   The time underneath Slide 1

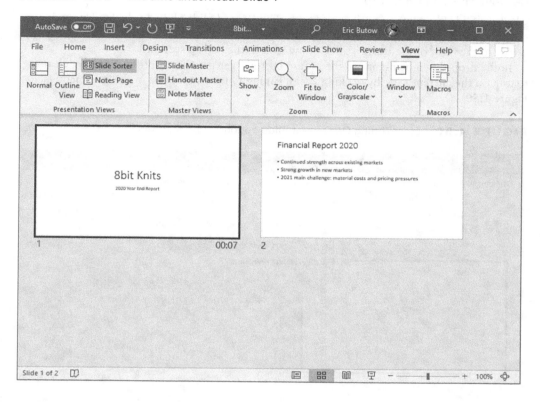

FIGURE 1.49   Manually button

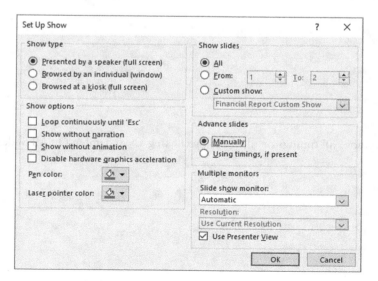

Remove the Timing Setup

Click the Slide Show menu option, and then click Record Slide Show in the Set Up section in the Slide Show ribbon. (If the width of your PowerPoint window is limited, click the down arrow to the right of the Record Slide Show icon in the Set Up section.)

In the drop-down menu, move the mouse button over the Clear option, and then clear the timing on the current slide by clicking Clear Timing On Current Slide in the side menu (see Figure 1.50).

FIGURE 1.50 Clear Timing On Current Slide option

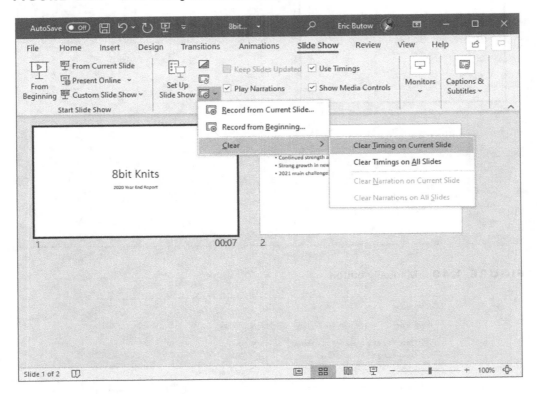

You can remove all timings on all slides by clicking Clear Timing On All Slides in the side menu.

Setting Up Slideshow Recording Options

An easier way to set your timings and make your presentation more professional is to narrate the audio for your presentation. In some cases, such as when you have an automated presentation in a kiosk, narration is a requirement if you want to use audio. You can also use recorded audio for presentations that people can view at any time, such as a new employee presentation that will be viewed by new employees over a period of months.

Record Audio Narration

Microsoft realized that you probably don't want to buy additional software to record your voice and then take that recording and import it into PowerPoint. Instead, you can record audio narration from within PowerPoint by following these steps:

1. Click the Slide Show menu option.
2. In the Set Up section in the Slide Show ribbon, click Record Slide Show. (If the width of your PowerPoint window is limited, click the down arrow to the right of the Record Slide Show icon in the Set Up section.)
3. Click Record From Beginning to start recording from the first slide (see Figure 1.51).

FIGURE 1.51   Record From Beginning option

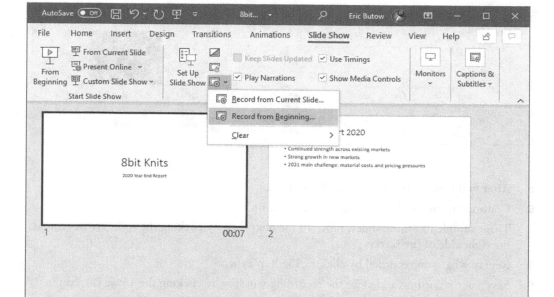

4. In the recording screen, shown in Figure 1.52, click Record, wait three seconds as PowerPoint counts down from three seconds down to zero, and then start speaking into your microphone.

FIGURE 1.52 Audio recording screen

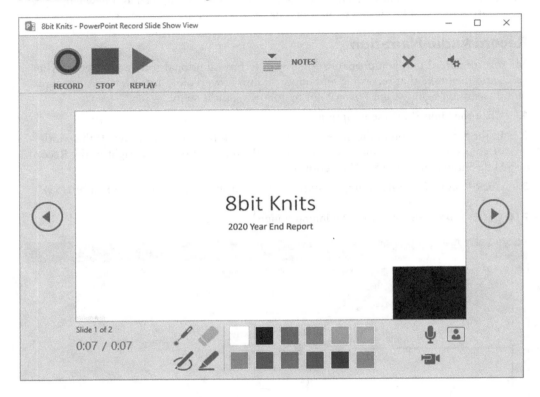

5. After you finish talking, click the Pause icon.
6. Continue recording by clicking the Record icon.
7. This example has three slides; move to the next slide by clicking the right arrow icon at the right side of the screen.
8. Replay what you recorded by clicking the Replay icon.
9. Save your recording and close the recording window by clicking the Close (X) icon in the upper-right corner of the window.

You return to the PowerPoint window in your previous view so that you can continue to work on your slideshow.

If your slides transition automatically, then PowerPoint turns off audio recording during the transition. There are two ways to get around this. The first is to stop speaking during the transition. The other way is to make all transitions manual, at least while you record, by changing the transition method to Manual, as you learned to do earlier in this chapter.

Your audio recording is not saved until you save the slideshow. You can do this by clicking the File menu option and then clicking Save on the File screen, or by pressing Ctrl+S.

Playing and Removing the Audio Recording

After you attach an audio recording to the slide, a black box appears in the lower-right corner of the slide. When you click the slide in Normal or Slide Sorter view and then move the mouse pointer over the black box, a playback bar appears (see Figure 1.53).

FIGURE 1.53 Playback bar

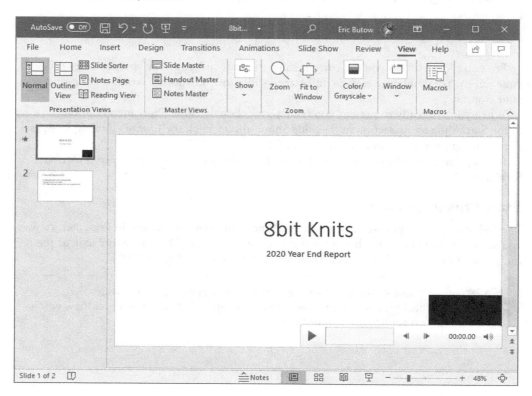

Play the audio by clicking the Play icon on the left side of the playback bar. If you decide that you don't like the audio and want to re-record it, you need to remove the audio and re-record it. (You can also remove the audio if you don't want it anymore.)

Click the black box within the slide. You know the audio recording box is selected when you see the sizing handles around the border of the box. There are two ways that you can delete the audio narration from the slide:

- Press Del (or Delete) on your keyboard to delete the audio from the slide.

- Click the Slide Show menu option, and then click Record Slide Show in the Set Up section in the Slide Show ribbon. In the drop-down menu, move the mouse button over the Clear option, and then clear the timing on the current slide by clicking Clear Narration On Current Slide in the side menu.

You can also delete audio narrations from all slides by clicking Clear Narrations On All Slides in the side menu.

Presenting Slideshows by Using Presenter View

When you present your slideshow, the Presenter View opens automatically and gives you an enhanced version of the PowerPoint interface, which PowerPoint calls speaker view, on one monitor.

Presenter View shows you the current slide, the next slide, and the speaker notes on your screen. Your audience sees the full-screen slideshow on another monitor connected to your computer.

When you are ready to present your slideshow, click the Slide Show menu option. In the Start Slide Show section in the Slide Show ribbon, click the From Beginning icon, as shown in Figure 1.54. (You can also press F5.)

If you prefer to start playing the slideshow from the current slide, click From Current Slide instead.

Start Presenter View

The full screen slide appears on your screen. When you move the mouse in Presenter View, you see a row of icons at the bottom-left corner of the screen. Click the More icon at the right side of the row, and then click Show Presenter View (see Figure 1.55).

These icons may be difficult to see, especially against a white background, so this may affect your decision to use Presenter View when presenting your slideshow.

FIGURE 1.54   From Beginning icon

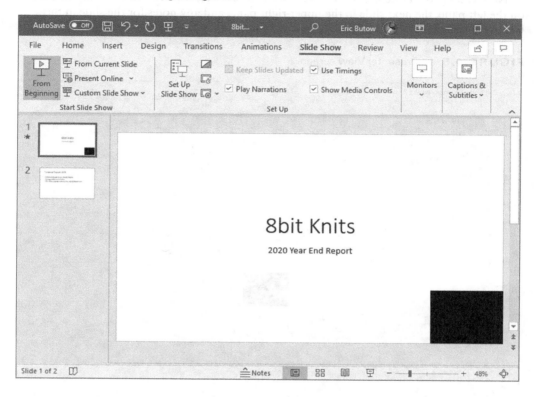

FIGURE 1.55   Full Screen View controls

Now you see the Presenter View screen (see Figure 1.56), which shows the current slide on the left pane, the next slide in the upper-right pane, and any notes for the slide in the lower-right pane.

FIGURE 1.56 Presenter View screen

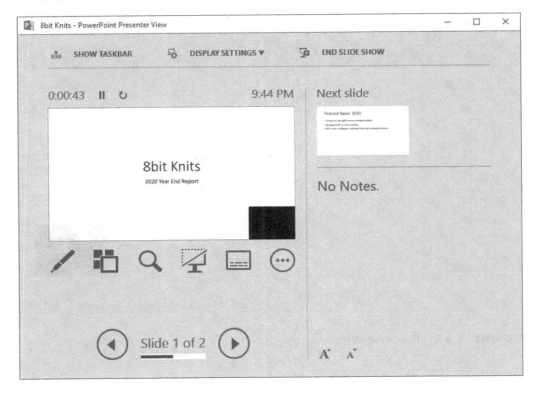

 The Presenter View screen is a separate screen within Windows. You can move between the Presenter View screen, full-screen slideshow screen, and the PowerPoint window by pressing Alt+Tab to switch between them.

Use Presenter View Controls

The main control options in Presenter View are in three areas: at the top of the screen, below the slide in the left pane, and at the bottom of the left pane.

Top of Screen

In the menu bar at the top of the screen, you can show and hide the Windows taskbar, change display settings, and end the slideshow.

 When you end the slideshow, you close both the Presenter View and full-screen slideshow screens and return to the PowerPoint window.

Below the Slide in the Left Pane

In the icon row just below the slide, click one of the following icons, from left to right:

- Change laser pointer and pen settings to annotate your slides.
- See a thumbnail view of all slides.
- Zoom into the slide.
- Make the entire slide black in case you want to hide it for any reason. Unhide the slide by clicking the icon again.
- Toggle subtitles on and off.
- View more options in the drop-down menu, including the ability to end the slideshow.

At the Bottom of the Left Pane

Click the left arrow icon to move to the previous slide, and click the right arrow icon to move to the next slide. The current slide number and total number of slides appear between the two arrow icons.

Set Monitor and Presenter View Settings

PowerPoint allows you to change the monitor settings and turn Presenter View on and off easily. Start by clicking the Slide Show menu option. In the Monitors section in the Slide Show ribbon, as shown in Figure 1.57, you can change one of the following options:

- In the Monitor area, click the Automatic box and then select the primary monitor to present your slideshow in the drop-down list.
- Clear the Use Presenter View check box to turn off Presenter View when you present a video. You can activate Presenter View by selecting the check box.

FIGURE 1.57   Monitors area in the Slide Show ribbon

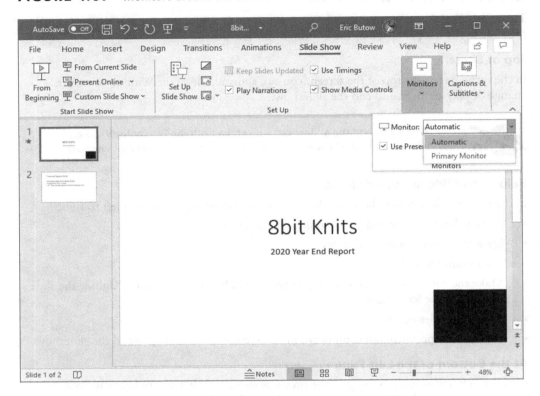

    If the width of your PowerPoint window is limited, click the Monitors icon and then select Automatic from the drop-down menu.

 **Real World Scenario**

Make Your Notes Bigger

You're getting close to giving your presentation when you become irritated by the small size of the Notes pane in the Presenter View. Fortunately, PowerPoint makes it easy to change the size of the pane as well as the size of the font so that you can focus on the notes and not the slides.

To perform both tasks, do the following:

1. Click the Slide Show menu option.

2. In the Slide Show ribbon, click the From Beginning icon.

3. On the full-screen presentation screen, click the More icon.

4. Select Show Presenter View from the drop-down menu.

5. Click and hold on the vertical line between the current slide and the notes. The cursor changes to a double-headed arrow.

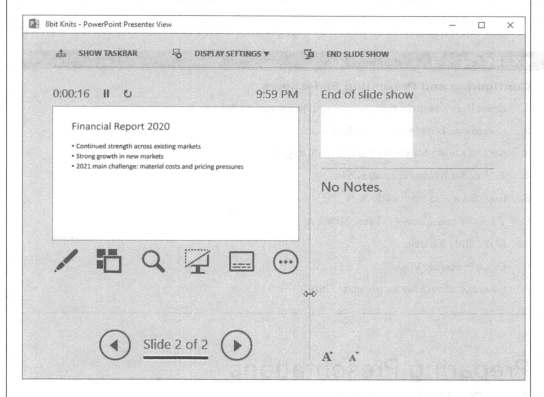

6. Drag the cursor to the left so that the notes are the size you want.

7. In the right pane, click and hold on the horizontal line between the slide above and the notes below. The cursor changes to an up and down double-headed arrow.

8. Drag the cursor up and down until the Notes pane is the size you want.

9. Click the Make The Text Larger icon (a large A) at the bottom of the Notes pane. Click this icon as many times as needed until the text size is somewhat larger than what you want.

10. Click the Make The Text Smaller icon (a smaller A) at the bottom of the Notes pane to shrink the size of the text. Click this icon as many times as needed until the text size is what you want.

Now that you have set the Notes pane and text size, close Presenter View. PowerPoint saves this setting so that you can use it with the current slideshow or a new slideshow.

EXERCISE 1.4

Configuring and Presenting Slideshows

1. Open the slideshow that you created in Exercise 1.3.

2. Create one bulleted list with four items.

3. Set the timing for slides 1 and 2 to 10 seconds.

4. Add audio narration to all slides.

5. Remove audio from slide 3.

6. View the slideshow in Presenter View.

7. Make slide 3 black.

8. Close Presenter View.

9. Save the slideshow by pressing Ctrl+S.

Preparing Presentations for Collaboration

PowerPoint makes it easy to share slideshows with other people, such as C-level executives in the company who need information displayed visually and succinctly.

Before you share your slideshow, you must finalize your presentation. If you share your presentations for review but you don't want people changing the presentation content, PowerPoint allows you to protect a slideshow with a password. You also need to check your slideshow for any issues that will prevent viewers from seeing your slideshow as you intend for it to be seen.

You can accept comments from reviewers within PowerPoint much as you do in a Word document. If you have slide masters in your slideshow but you don't want PowerPoint to delete them because you plan to use them when you add slides later, you can preserve those slide masters. When you're ready to share your slideshow, you can export the slideshow to other formats as well as external media, including CDs and USB drives.

Mark Presentations as Final

Before you prepare your presentation to share with others, take care to mark the presentation as final. When you or someone else opens a file, a yellow warning bar appears below the menu bar that tells you the presentation has been marked as final to discourage any further editing.

Here's how to mark your presentation as final:

1. Click the File menu option.

2. Click Info in the menu bar on the left side of the File screen.

3. On the Info screen, click the Protect Presentation button.

4. Select Mark As Final from the drop-down menu (see Figure 1.58).

FIGURE 1.58   Mark As Final option

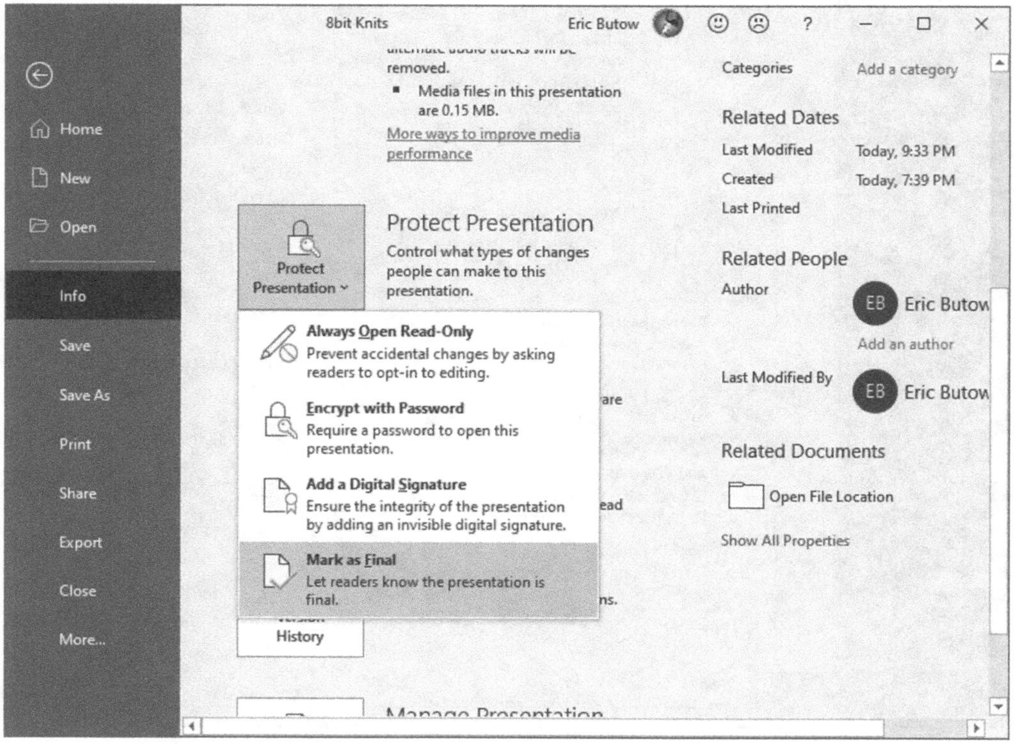

5. Click OK in the dialog box.

6. In the dialog box that tells you the slideshow has been marked as final, click OK.

The yellow warning bar appears below the menu bar. The warning bar appears every time that you open the file.

Protecting Presentations by Using Passwords

Unfortunately, anyone can edit a slideshow marked as final by clicking the Edit Anyway button in the warning bar, or by simply going to the Info screen and selecting Mark As Final from the Protect Presentation drop-down menu. You can secure your slideshow from edits by adding a password to your PowerPoint file.

Follow these steps to add a password:

1. Click the File menu option.

2. Click Info in the menu bar on the left side of the File screen.

3. On the Info screen, click the Protect Presentation button.

4. Select Encrypt With Password from the drop-down menu, as shown in Figure 1.59.

FIGURE 1.59 Encrypt With Password option

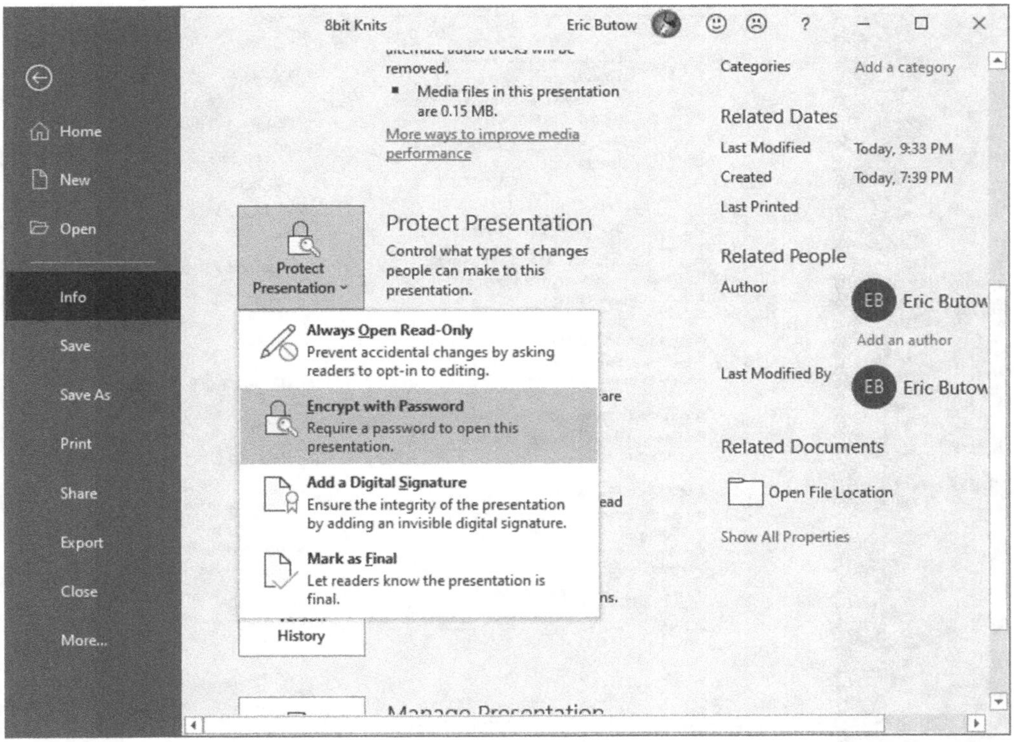

5. In the Encrypt Document dialog box, type the case-sensitive password in the Password box (see Figure 1.60).

FIGURE 1.60   Encrypt Document dialog box

6. Click OK.

7. In the Confirm Password dialog box, type the password again in the Reenter Password box.

8. Click OK.

The Protect Presentation option on the Info screen is highlighted in yellow to let you know that a password is required to open the presentation.

Apply the password by clicking Save in the menu on the left side of the PowerPoint window.

If you decide that you don't want a password, repeat steps 1–4. Then, in the Encrypt Document dialog box, delete the password in the Password box and then click OK. The Protect Presentation option is no longer highlighted in yellow, so now you know the slideshow is not password protected.

Inspecting Presentations for Issues

Before you share a slideshow with other people, such as in an email attachment, you should take advantage of the Document Inspector in PowerPoint to find information that you may not realize is saved with your slideshow. For example, PowerPoint saves author information, and you may not want to share that information when you share the slideshow with someone outside your company.

Before you inspect your slideshow and perhaps remove some information, you may want to save a copy of your slideshow and remove the information from that copy. PowerPoint may not be able to restore data when you click Undo in the Quick Access Toolbar or press Ctrl+Z, so it's better to be safe than sorry.

Start by clicking the File menu option. Click Info in the menu bar on the left side of the File screen. Now that you're on the Info screen, click the Check For Issues button. From the drop-down list, select Inspect Document.

If you haven't saved your slideshow, a dialog box will appear that prompts you to do so. Click Yes to save the slideshow.

Now you see the Document Inspector dialog box, as shown in Figure 1.61. Scroll up and down the list of content that Windows will inspect.

FIGURE 1.61 Document Inspector dialog box

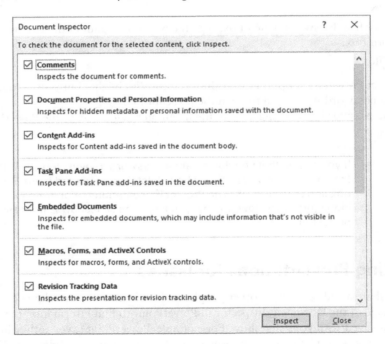

By default, the following check boxes next to the content category names are selected:

- Comments
- Document Properties And Personal Information
- Content Add-Ins
- Task Pane Add-Ins
- Embedded Documents
- Macros, Forms, And ActiveX Controls
- Revision Tracking Data
- Custom XML Data
- Invisible On-Slide Content (This is content on slides that has been formatted not to show up on the slide, such as white text on a white background, but it does not include objects covered by other objects.)
- Presentation Notes

These check boxes mean that the Document Inspector will check content in all those areas.

Select the Ink check box if you want to check whether someone has written in the slideshow with a stylus, such as the Microsoft Surface Pen. If you want to check for invisible objects that are not visible because they are outside the slide area (excluding animated objects), select Off-Slide Content.

When you decide what you want PowerPoint to check out, click Inspect. Once PowerPoint finishes its inspection, you can review all the results in the dialog box.

The results show all content categories that look good by displaying a green check mark to the left of the category name. If PowerPoint finds something that you should check out, you see a red exclamation point to the left of the category. Under the category name, PowerPoint lists everything it found. Remove the offenders from your slideshow by clicking the Remove All button to the right of the category name.

You can reinspect the slideshow by clicking Reinspect as often as you want until you see that all the categories are okay. When you're done, click the Close button to return to the Info screen.

Adding and Managing Comments

During the review process, other people (and even you) may want to add comments to the slideshow. A comment is an easy way to get the attention of reviewers without affecting text or images in slides. Comments appear in a slide as a text bubble icon.

Insert Comments

Here's how to insert a comment into a slideshow:

1. Select the text or image on the slide on which you want to comment.
2. Click the Review menu option.
3. In the Review menu ribbon, click New Comment in the Comments section.

PowerPoint shows your comment with a red outline in the Comments pane on the right side of the PowerPoint window (see Figure 1.62).

FIGURE 1.62   A new comment

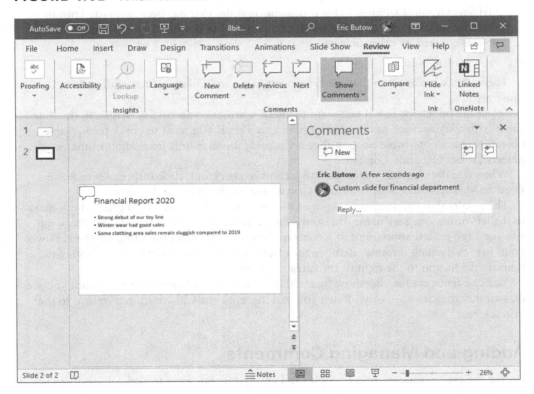

The red outline represents the default color of the primary reviewer. (That's you.) Power-Point assigns different colors to different commenters automatically. When you finish typing the comment, press Enter. The comment appears in the margin. You can type a new comment by clicking the New button at the top of the Comments pane.

At the top of the comment box, PowerPoint displays your Microsoft 365 username, your avatar, and how long ago you wrote the comment. An avatar is an icon that you created for yourself when you created a Microsoft 365 account. If you don't have one, then PowerPoint shows a placeholder avatar.

View, Review, and Reply to Comments

When you want to view a comment, you can click on the text bubble icon in the slide to open the Comments pane (if it isn't already open) and view the associated comment. Selected comment icons in a slide have a solid color background, such as red. A comment that is not selected has an icon with a white background.

You can review comments by scrolling through the slideshow, but you can also use the Review menu ribbon to go to the next comment. Start by clicking the Review menu option. In the Review menu ribbon, click Next in the Comments section to see the next comment in the Comments pane (see Figure 1.63).

FIGURE 1.63   The next comment

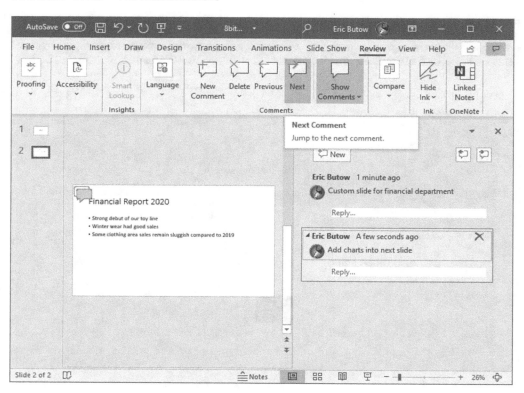

PowerPoint takes you to the slide that contains the next comment in the document. Go to the previous comment in the slideshow by clicking Previous in the ribbon, as shown in Figure 1.63.

If you see a comment from someone else (or even yourself) and you want to reply, click Reply in the comment box and then enter your reply. When you're finished, click in the document. You see the reply indented underneath the first comment.

 Anyone who can access your slideshow can edit your comments, not just the information in each slide.

Delete Comments

Here's how to delete one or more comments when you decide that you no longer need them:

1. Click in the comment box.
2. Click the Review menu option, if necessary.
3. In the Review menu ribbon, click the Delete icon in the Comments section (see Figure 1.64).

FIGURE 1.64 Deleting a comment

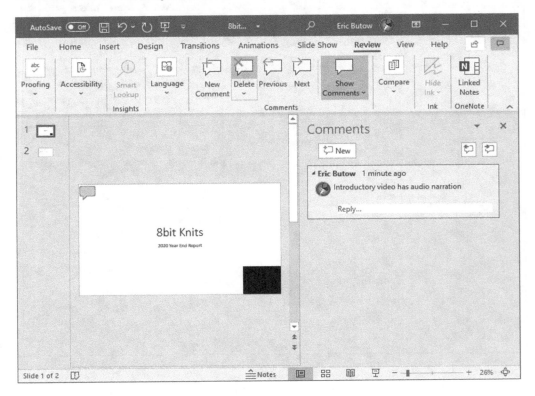

PowerPoint deletes the comment and any replies within that comment.

You can delete all comments in the slideshow, even without selecting a comment, by clicking the down arrow underneath the Delete icon in the ribbon. From the drop-down menu, select Delete All Comments In This Presentation. After you click Yes in the dialog box that appears, all comments in the slideshow disappear.

Print One or More Comments

When you want to print one or more comments for yourself or share with someone else, follow these steps:

1. Click the File menu option.
2. Click Print in the menu bar on the left side of the File screen.
3. On the Print screen, click the Full Page Slides button.
4. Select Print Comments from the drop-down list, as shown in Figure 1.65.

FIGURE 1.65 Print Comments option

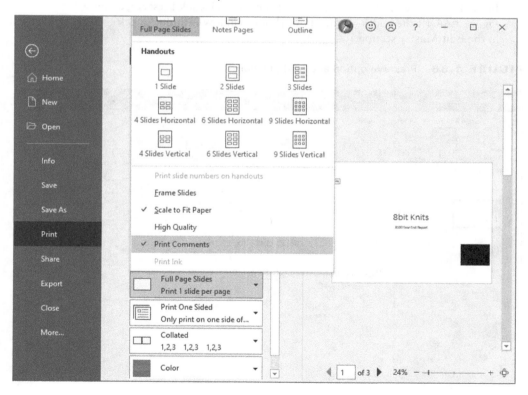

PowerPoint may have this option checked by default; in that case you can click Print Comments to remove the check mark if you don't want to print comments with your slideshow.

Once you ensure that Print Comments is on, you can print the slideshow and all comments by clicking the Print button on the Print screen.

Preserving Presentation Content

Over time, PowerPoint will try to be helpful and delete any master slides that the program detects you haven't used for a while. If you want to keep a master slide for use later, Power-Point allows you to preserve the slide master, which tells the program not to delete it.

Preserve the master by following these steps:

1. Click the View menu option.

2. In the Master Views section in the View ribbon, click Slide Master.

3. Click the master slide that you want to preserve in the left pane.

4. In the Edit Master section in the Slide Master ribbon, click Preserve, as shown in Figure 1.66. (If the width of your PowerPoint window is limited, click the Preserve icon in the Edit Master section.)

FIGURE 1.66   Preserve option and pushpin icon

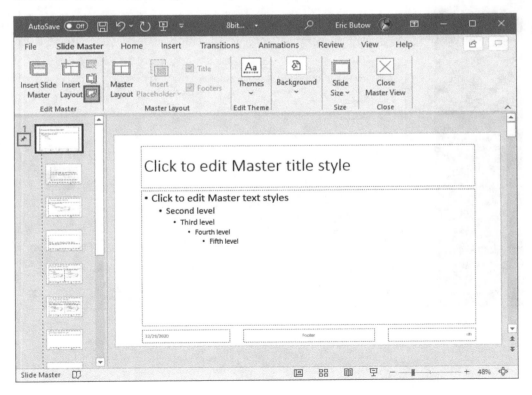

A pushpin icon appears to the left of the slide master, as you can see in Figure 1.66. Now you can rest easier knowing that PowerPoint won't try to help you and automatically delete that slide master.

Exporting Presentations to Other Formats

If you want to share your slideshow with other people but they want to have it in a different format, such as a video file, PowerPoint makes it easy to export your slideshow to video as well as many other formats.

Start by clicking the File menu option, and then click Export in the menu bar on the left side of the File screen. On the Export screen, shown in Figure 1.67, you can click one of the six export options.

FIGURE 1.67   Export options on the Export screen

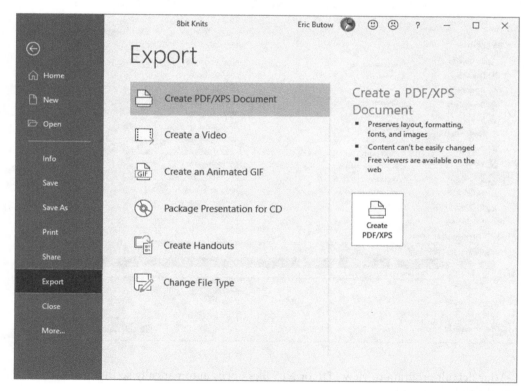

Export to a PDF or XPS Document

The Create PDF/XPS Document option is selected by default. You can export to the Adobe PDF format or the Open XML Paper Specification, better known by its file extension .xps.

Here's how to export the file to PDF or XPS:

1. Click the Create PDF/XPS button, which you saw in Figure 1.67.

2. In the Publish As PDF Or XPS dialog box, navigate to the folder where you want to save the file. The filename of the slideshow is the default filename in the File Name box.

3. In the Save As Type area, click the PDF button and then select either PDF or XPS Document from the drop-down list, as shown in Figure 1.68. (If you want PDF, then you can skip this step.)

4. Click Publish.

FIGURE 1.68   Save As Type drop-down list

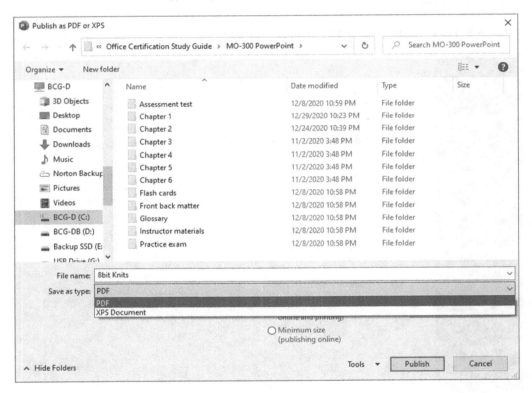

Your default program to view PDF or XPS files opens automatically so that you can see how the slideshow looks.

Export a Slideshow as a Video

Click Create A Video on the Export screen to view the Create A Video export options (see Figure 1.69).

FIGURE 1.69 Video export options

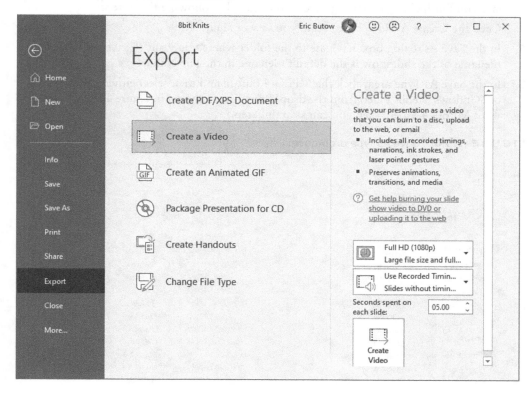

You can click one of the following three boxes to change how your slideshow is exported to a video:

Full HD (1080p)   Change the video resolution, which by default is 1080p. From the drop-down menu, you can select Standard (480p), HD (720p), or Ultra HD (4K). Each option includes the pixel dimensions for each setting.

Use Recorded Timings And Narrations   The exported video file will include the slide timings and the audio narrations contained in the slideshow. You can turn this option off by selecting Don't Use Recorded Timings And Narrations, which means that the exported video will use PowerPoint default timing settings and will not export audio narrations.

Seconds Spent On Each Slide   If you don't use recorded timings but want to have a custom time spent on each slide, this box shows a default of five seconds on each slide. Type the number of seconds as precise as to the hundredths of a second in the box, or click the up and down arrows to increase and decrease, respectively, the time by one second.

Once you finish changing settings, create the video by following these steps:

1. Click the Create A Video button that you saw in Figure 1.69.

2. In the Save As dialog box, navigate to the folder where you want to save the file. The filename of the slideshow is the default filename in the File Name box.

3. In the Save As Type area, click the MPEG-4 button and then select either MPEG-4 Video or Windows Media Video from the drop-down list, as shown in Figure 1.70. (If you want MPEG-4 Video, then you can skip this step.)

FIGURE 1.70   Save As Type drop-down list

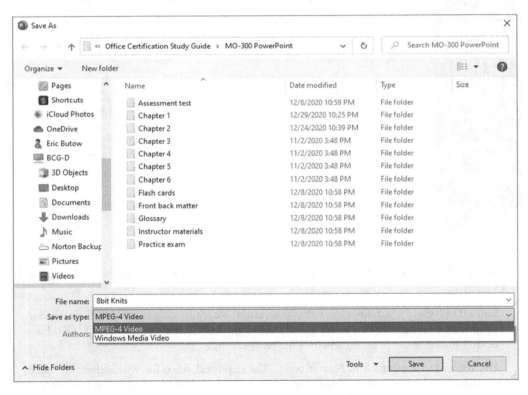

4. Click Save.

You need to open File Explorer and navigate to the folder with the video file to double-click the file and view it in your default video player program.

 The next option in the Export list is Create An Animated GIF, but that task is not covered on the MO-300 exam.

Package a Presentation to Save to a CD-R or CD-RW

If you want to package a slideshow to save to a recordable compact disc (CD-R) or compact disc rewritable (CD-RW)—for example, when you want someone to take home a copy of the presentation so that they can view it on their computer at their leisure—PowerPoint allows you to burn your slideshow directly to a CD-R or CD-RW.

After you insert a blank CD-R or CD-RW and navigate to the File screen, as you learned to do earlier in this chapter, follow these steps:

1. Click Package Presentation For CD on the Export screen.
2. Click the Package For CD button, as shown in Figure 1.71.

FIGURE 1.71   Package For CD button

3. In the Package For CD dialog box, shown in Figure 1.72, select the default PresentationCD name in the Name The CD box and type in a new CD name.

FIGURE 1.72   Package For CD dialog box

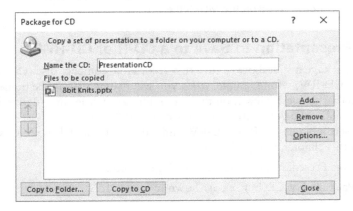

4. For this example, leave the current slideshow file in the Files To Be Copied area as is without clicking any other options and then click Copy To CD.

5. In the dialog box, include all linked files on the CD by clicking Yes.

6. After PowerPoint copies your slideshow to the CD, click Close in the Package For CD dialog box.

In the Package For CD dialog box, you can also package your slideshow to be placed in another folder, such as on your company intranet or a USB drive.

Click Copy To Folder in the dialog box, and then change the presentation name and browse to a new folder location if necessary. When you click OK, PowerPoint publishes your slideshow and opens the folder in the File Explorer window.

Create Handouts

If you want to edit and format your handouts in Word before you present them to others, you can export the handout files to Word directly within PowerPoint.

After you open the Export screen, as you learned to do earlier in this chapter, click Create Handouts in the menu and then click the Create Handouts button, as shown in Figure 1.73.

FIGURE 1.73   Create Handouts button

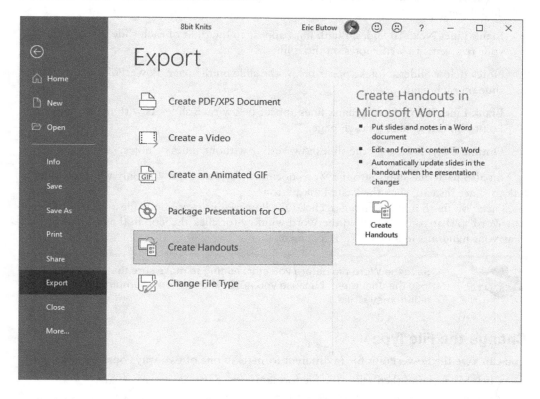

In the Send To Microsoft Word dialog box, shown in Figure 1.74, you can set up your handout page layout in one of five ways:

FIGURE 1.74   Send To Microsoft Word dialog box

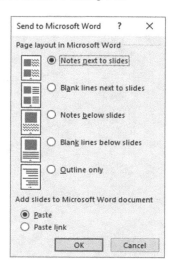

Notes Next To Slides: Notes appear to the right of each slide on the page. This is the default setting.

Blank Lines Next To Slides: Blank lines appear to the right of each slide if you want your recipients to write notes on those lines.

Notes Below Slides: Notes appear below the slide on the page. PowerPoint places one slide on each page.

Blank Lines Below Slides: Blank lines appear below each slide. As with notes, Power-Point places one slide on each page.

Outline Only: Print only the slideshow outline without slides or notes.

You also paste the slides into the Word document by default. If you only want to export a link to slides instead, click the Paste Link button.

When you finish making changes, click OK. PowerPoint exports the file and opens Micro-soft Word so that you can click in the Word window (or click the icon in the taskbar) and view your handouts in a new Word document.

 Save the Word file before you start editing to make sure that you don't lose the document, because you never know when a computer or power failure may strike.

Change the File Type

You can save the PowerPoint file in different formats in one of two ways on the File screen:

- Click Save As and then select the file format on the Save As screen.

- Click Export and then click Change File Type on the Export screen. A list of common presentation and image file types appears in the Change File Type list, as shown in Figure 1.75.

FIGURE 1.75   Change File Type list

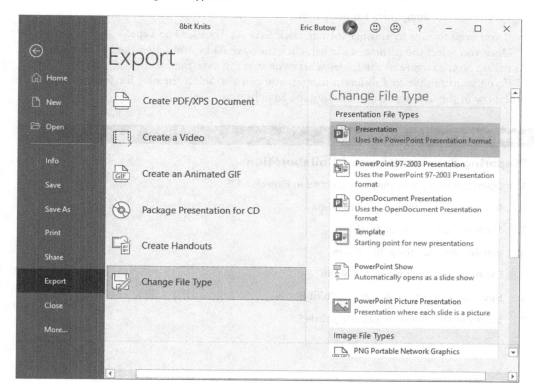

The default file type is Presentation, which is a current PowerPoint file. You can also save the file in seven other formats:

- PowerPoint 97-2003 Presentation for older versions of PowerPoint
- An OpenDocument Presentation
- A PowerPoint template to use as the basis for other slideshows
- PowerPoint Show to open the PowerPoint file automatically as a slideshow
- A PowerPoint Picture Presentation where PowerPoint saves each slide as its own picture file

- PNG-format image files for each slide
- JPEG-format image files for each slide

If you need to save to another format, click Save As Another File Type.

Once you select the format in the list, click the Save As button under the list. In the Save As dialog box, navigate to the folder where you want to save the file.

If you want to save to a different format, you can also select the new file format. Save the slideshow in the new format by clicking the Save button.

EXERCISE 1.5

Preparing Presentations for Collaboration

1. Open the slideshow that you created in Exercise 1.3.

2. Add two comments to the first slide.

3. Mark the slideshow as final.

4. Inspect the slideshow for issues.

5. Export the slideshow as a PDF file.

6. Save the slideshow as a PowerPoint Show.

7. Save the slideshow by pressing Ctrl+S.

Summary

This chapter started by showing you how to change the slide master theme and background in PowerPoint. Then you saw how to modify content in a slide master. You learned how to create and modify slide layouts. You also learned how to modify handouts and notes masters.

After you created and modified masters, you learned how to change the slide size. Next, you saw how to display your presentation in one of five different views. You also learned how to find and change basic properties in your PowerPoint file.

Then you learned how to print all or part of a slideshow, notes pages, and handouts. You also saw how to tell PowerPoint to print a slideshow in color, grayscale, or pure black and white.

Next, I discussed how to create a custom slideshow. You learned how to configure your slideshow options. After that, I discussed how to rehearse your slideshow timing and set up slideshow recording options. You also learned how to present slideshows in Presenter View.

Finally, you learned several important things about preparing your slideshow to share with others, including marking a slideshow as final, using a password to prevent edits, inspecting presentations for issues, adding and managing comments, preserving slide masters, and exporting a slideshow to other formats.

Key Terms

handouts	presentation
layouts	slide master
masters	slideshow
notes	theme
placeholder areas	timing

Exam Essentials

Understand how to modify slide masters.   Know how to select a prebuilt theme for your slide master as well as how to change the background of a slide master whether you applied a theme to the master or not.

Know how to create and modify slide layouts.   Understand how to create a layout within a master slide, how to add more placeholder areas within a layout, and how to rename and delete a layout.

Understand how to modify handout and notes masters.   Know how to format handout and notes masters, and understand why these masters are different from style masters.

Know how to change the slide size.   Understand how to change the size of a slide between the built-in standard and widescreen sizes, as well as how to resize your content to a resized slide.

Understand how to display presentations in different views.   Know how to use the five built-in PowerPoint views to display a slideshow in the way that you want.

Be able to set basic file properties.   Know how to open the Info screen, view the properties of your PowerPoint file, and make changes to various properties, such as tags and categories.

Know how to print all or part of a presentation.   Understand how to print an entire slideshow or specific slides within the slideshow.

Understand how to print notes pages and handouts.   Know how to print notes and handouts from the Print screen.

Know how to print in color, grayscale, and black and white.   Understand how to tell PowerPoint to print in color, grayscale, or black and white, no matter what type of printer you have.

Understand how to create custom slideshows.   Know how to create a custom slideshow that you can present only to certain audiences, as well as how to connect a custom slideshow with an existing slideshow.

Be able to configure slideshow options.   Know how to select the right slideshow option between the default Show Type as well as how to change show options, show slides, advance slides, and use multiple monitors connected to your computer.

Know how to rehearse slideshow timing.   Know how to rehearse the timing between slides so that you can ensure that the slides move when you expect them to move during your presentation, or to synchronize your slides with your audio narration.

Understand how to set up slideshow recording.   Know how to record audio narration within PowerPoint, play your recent audio recording, and delete the narration if you don't like it.

Know how to present slideshows in Presenter View.   Understand how to open Presenter View and use the controls in Presenter View, such as to make the notes area larger when you present your slideshow to an audience.

Understand how to mark presentations as final.   Know why you need to mark a slideshow as final, how to mark your slideshow as final, and the limitations of marking a slideshow as final.

Know how to use passwords to keep others from editing your slideshow.   Understand how to enter a password in your PowerPoint file to keep reviewers from editing text and images in the slideshow.

Understand how to inspect presentations for issues.   Know how to use the Document Inspector to inspect your slideshow for any issues that could cause problems viewing the slideshow for some people who view it.

Be able to add and manage comments.   Know how to add comments and manage comments added to your slideshow by reviewers.

Know how to preserve slide masters.   Understand why you need to preserve an inactive slide master so that PowerPoint does not delete it automatically.

Understand how to export presentations to other formats.   Know how to export your slideshow to other presentation, graphic, and documentation formats, such as PDF.

Review Questions

1. What are some options for changing a slide layout? (Choose all that apply.)
   - **A.** Fonts
   - **B.** Themes
   - **C.** Colors
   - **D.** Headers

2. What view does PowerPoint use by default?
   - **A.** Reading view
   - **B.** Normal
   - **C.** Outline view
   - **D.** Notes Page

3. When you type **3-8,10,12** in the Slides box within the Print menu, what slides does Power-Point print? (Choose all that apply.)
   - **A.** All slides from 3 through 12
   - **B.** Slides 3 through 8
   - **C.** Slides 10 through 12
   - **D.** Slides 10 and 12

4. When you want to set up a slideshow so that it loops continuously, what section in the Set Up Show dialog box must you go to?
   - **A.** Advance Slides
   - **B.** Show Options
   - **C.** Show Type
   - **D.** Show Slides

5. Why would you protect a slideshow with a password instead of marking a slideshow as final?
   - **A.** You need to mark a slideshow as final before you can add a password.
   - **B.** Marking and saving with a password are the same thing.
   - **C.** Because PowerPoint won't allow you to share a document until you add a password
   - **D.** Because marking a slideshow still gives others the ability to edit the slideshow

6. What happens when you apply changes to a handout master?
   - **A.** The handout pages remain the same until you apply the master.
   - **B.** A dialog box appears asking if you want to apply the changes to all handout pages.
   - **C.** PowerPoint applies the changes to all pages in the handout.
   - **D.** PowerPoint does not apply the changes until you save the slideshow.

7. What are the standard slide sizes? (Choose all that apply.)

   A. Standard (4:3)

   B. On-screen Show (16:10)

   C. Overhead

   D. Widescreen (16:9)

8. How many handout print options can you choose from?

   A. Five

   B. Nine

   C. Eight

   D. Six

9. In Presenter View, where do you look to see what slide you're on?

   A. In the top menu bar

   B. At the top of the left pane

   C. At the bottom of the left pane

   D. In the top-right pane

10. What are the video resolutions that you can select when you export a slideshow to a video? (Choose all that apply.)

   A. HD (720p)

   B. Standard (4:3)

   C. 1080p

   D. Widescreen (16:9)

Chapter

2

Managing Slides

MICROSOFT EXAM OBJECTIVES COVERED IN THIS CHAPTER:

✓ **Manage slides**

- Insert slides
  - Import Word document outlines
  - Insert slides from another presentation
  - Insert slides and select slide layouts
  - Insert Summary Zoom slides
  - Duplicate slides
- Modify slides
  - Hide and unhide slides
  - Modify individual slide backgrounds
  - Insert slide headers, footers, and page numbers
- Order and group slides
  - Create sections
  - Modify slide order
  - Rename sections

Chapter 1, "Creating Presentations," contained information about how to modify slide masters and a high-level overview of how to set up a slideshow. In this chapter, I will take a deeper dive into the various ways of inserting slides into a slideshow.

I will then show you how to modify slides by hiding and unhiding slides, modifying backgrounds in individual slides, as well as inserting headers and footers into slides, including page numbers.

Finally, I will show you how you can change the order of your slides and add sections so that you can group related slides. You will also learn how to rename sections to match what the slides in the section are about.

At the end of each section in this chapter, I will provide an exercise so that you can test yourself and see if you can apply what you've learned.

Inserting Slides

Microsoft PowerPoint allows you to insert slides in a variety of ways. You can import an outline that you created in Word into PowerPoint and build your presentation from there. If you want to use slides from another presentation in your current one, you can reuse slides. You can also add a blank slide yourself and apply a layout to it before you start editing the slide.

Once you insert your slides and order them in the way you want, you can use the Summary Zoom feature to go to different slides quickly as you give your presentation. And when you need to duplicate one or more existing slides within your presentation to speed up the creation process, PowerPoint has a built-in tool to do that, too.

Importing Word Document Outlines

If you create an outline in Word that you want to use in a presentation, such as an outline for a report that needs to be presented to the board of directors, PowerPoint allows you to import an outline directly from Word. Here's how to do that:

1. Open a new or existing presentation in PowerPoint.

2. Click the slide where you want to insert a new slide. That new slide will appear after your selected slide.

3. Click the Home menu option (if necessary).

4. In the Slides section in the Home ribbon, click New Slide. (If the PowerPoint window has a small width, click Slides in the ribbon and then select New Slide from the drop-down menu.)

5. Select Slides From Outline from the drop-down menu, as shown in Figure 2.1.

FIGURE 2.1   Slides From Outline option at the bottom of the drop-down menu

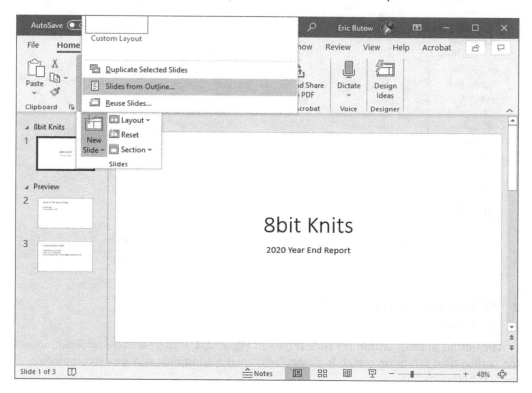

6. In the Insert Outline dialog box, shown in Figure 2.2, navigate to the folder that contains the outline.

FIGURE 2.2   Insert Outline dialog box

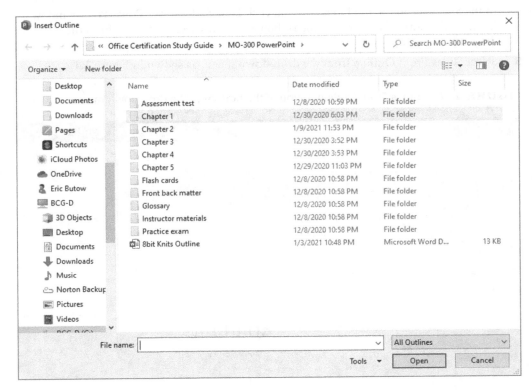

7. Click the filename in the list.

8. Click Insert.

The outline appears within the slide shown in Figure 2.3. If there is more information in the outline than can fit on one slide, PowerPoint creates additional slides to accommodate the text automatically.

Within Word, you can create the outline in Outline view or as paragraphs with heading styles. You can save a document in Outline view, just as you can with any other document.

If the outline is in paragraph form and contains no heading style, PowerPoint creates a slide for each paragraph in the Word outline.

FIGURE 2.3   The outline appears within the slide.

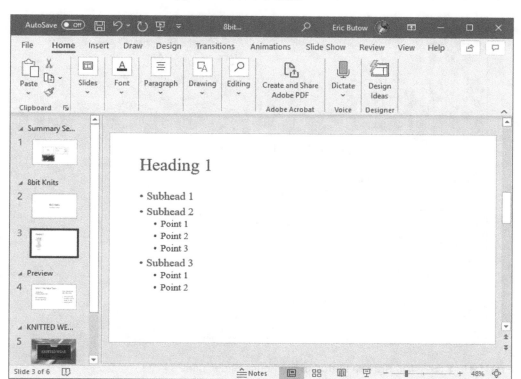

Inserting Slides from Another Presentation

When you have slides in another presentation that you want to use, such as notes about the confidentiality of the information, you can reuse slides from another presentation. Follow these steps:

1. Open a new or existing presentation in PowerPoint.

2. Click the slide below which you want to insert the slide from the other presentation.

3. Click the Home menu option (if necessary).

4. In the Slides section in the Home ribbon, click New Slide. (If the PowerPoint window has a small width, click Slides in the ribbon and then select New Slide from the drop-down menu.)

5. Select Reuse Slides from the drop-down menu, as shown in Figure 2.4.

6. In the Reuse Slides pane at the right side of the PowerPoint window (see Figure 2.5), click the Browse button.

FIGURE 2.4   Reuse Slides option at the bottom of the drop-down menu

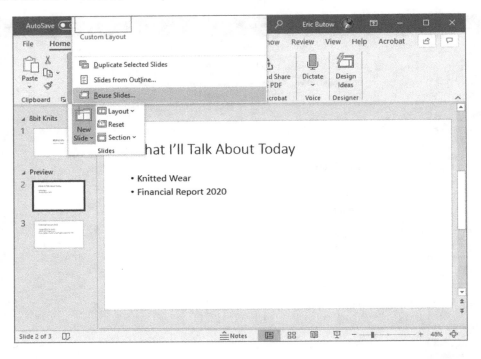

FIGURE 2.5   The Browse button in the Reuse Slides pane

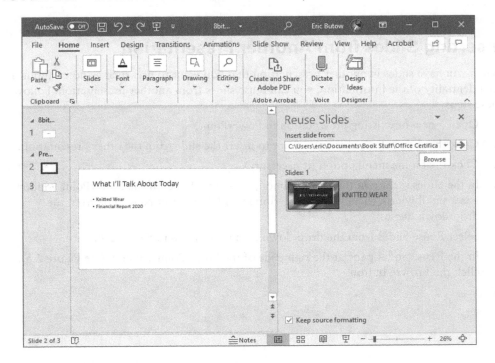

7. In the Browse dialog box, navigate to the folder that contains the PowerPoint file, click the filename, and then click Open.

8. Select the Keep Source Formatting check box to keep the format of the slide.

9. Click the slide in the Reuse Slides pane.

The inserted slide with its source formatting appears after the selected slide, as shown in Figure 2.6.

FIGURE 2.6   The inserted slide

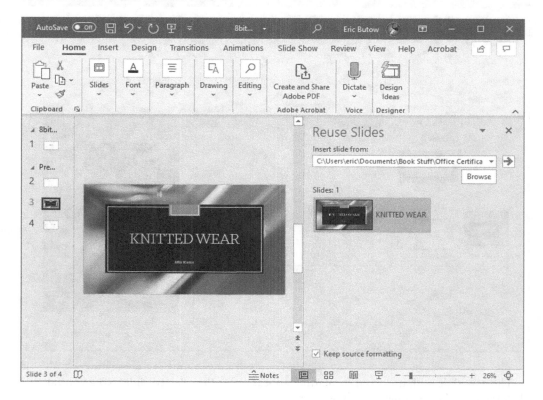

Now you can close the Reuse Slides pane by clicking the Close (X) icon in the upper-right corner of the pane.

Inserting Slides and Selecting Slide Layouts

When you just want to insert a blank slide and then apply an existing slide layout to it, follow these steps:

1. Click the slide below which you want to insert the new slide.

2. Click the Home menu option, if necessary.

3. In the Slides section in the Home ribbon, click New Slide. (If the PowerPoint window has a small width, click Slides in the ribbon and then select New Slide from the drop-down menu.)

4. In the drop-down list (see Figure 2.7), click the slide layout icon.

FIGURE 2.7 Slide layout icons in the list

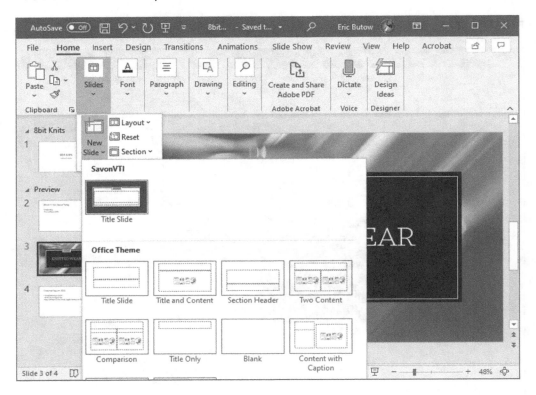

The new slide with its layout formatting appears after the selected slide. Now you can click the new slide and make changes to it.

If you reused a slide that has a different layout, that layout also appears within the list shown in Figure 2.7.

Inserting Summary Zoom Slides

When you need to see all of your slides at once and display a specific slide during your presentation, such as a slide that will reinforce a point you're trying to make when answering a question, you can create a *Summary Zoom* slide. Here's how:

1. Click the Insert menu option.
2. In the Links section in the Insert ribbon, click Zoom. (If the PowerPoint window has a small width, click Links in the ribbon and then select Zoom from the drop-down menu.)
3. Select Summary Zoom from the drop-down menu, as shown in Figure 2.8.

FIGURE 2.8   The Summary Zoom option

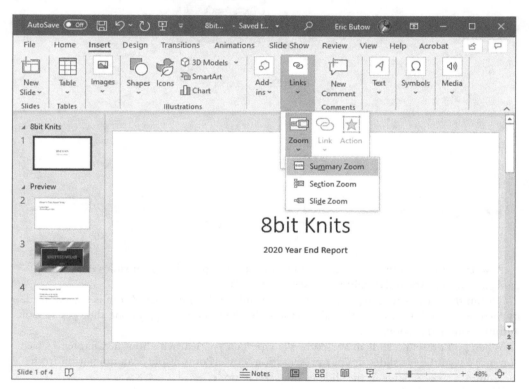

4. In the Insert Summary Zoom dialog box (see Figure 2.9), click all the slides that you want to add to your Summary Zoom slide. As you click each slide, the check box underneath the thumbnail-sized slide is selected.

5. Click Insert.

FIGURE 2.9   Insert Summary Zoom dialog box

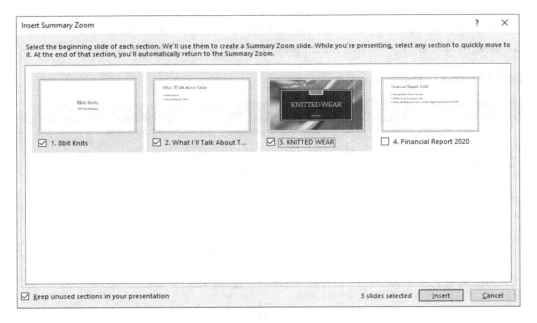

PowerPoint creates the Summary Zoom slide at the top of the list of slides in the left pane, and it appears in the right pane (see Figure 2.10).

Within the list of slides in the left pane, each slide in the Summary Zoom is placed inside its own section with a section title above the slide. PowerPoint displays one slide per section within a Summary Zoom slide.

When you present a slide in Presenter View (which you learned about in Chapter 1), as you move to different slides in your presentation, PowerPoint displays an animation from the Summary Zoom slide in the slide in full-screen mode.

The downside to this approach is that once you move to the next slide, you go back to the Summary Zoom slide, so click the Next icon in the icon row in the lower left of the screen, press Page Down, or press the down arrow on your keyboard to move to the next slide.

FIGURE 2.10 The Summary Zoom slide in the right pane

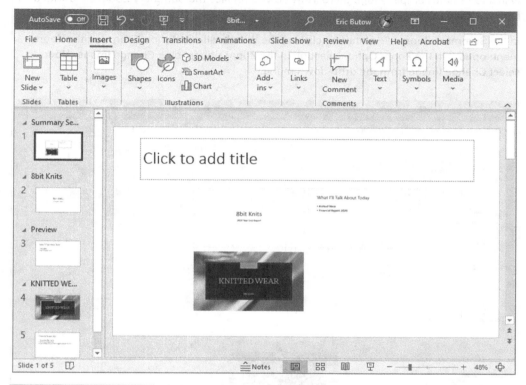

 If you don't include a slide within the Summary Zoom slides, that slide is still a part of your presentation. However, any slides excluded from the Summary Zoom slide are not included in a section unless you click and drag that excluded slide underneath a section name. In that case, any slides below the excluded slide within the section are no longer included in the Zoom slide.

 **Real World Scenario**

Changing a Summary Zoom Slide to an Image

Your boss likes the Summary Zoom slide as a way for potential new clients to understand why they should buy from your company. But the opening slide is just text, and your boss wants to see the company logo there. How do you replace the Summary Zoom slide with a logo but keep the original slide as text?

In the Summary Zoom slide, start by clicking the thumbnail-sized slide. Then click the Zoom menu option. In the Zoom Options section in the Zoom ribbon, click Change Image. Now select Change Image from the drop-down menu.

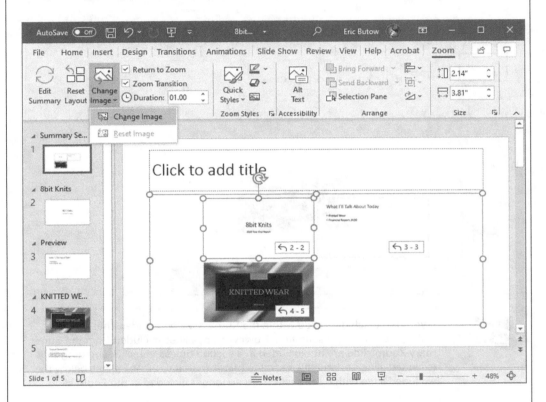

In the Insert Pictures dialog box, you can insert a picture from a file, a picture from stock images, an online picture from cloud-based storage services like OneDrive, or a picture from the PowerPoint icon collection.

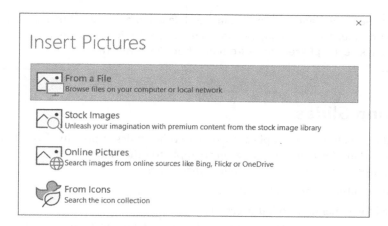

The next dialog box you see depends on the type of picture you add. Once you add a picture, it replaces the text thumbnail-sized slide in the Summary Zoom slide. However, when you look at the slide in the left pane, the slide still has text in it, and when you click that slide, it appears in the right pane.

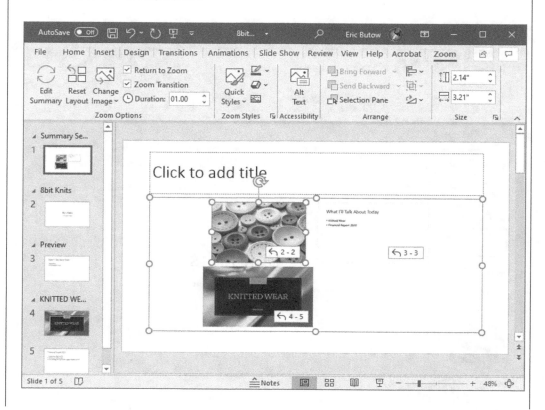

You can delete the picture and display text in the slide again by clicking the picture in the Summary Zoom slide, clicking Change Image in the Zoom Options section in the Zoom ribbon, and then selecting Reset Image from the drop-down menu.

Duplicating Slides

You may find that you want to duplicate a slide to other slides, especially if you have the same background and/or text that you want to apply to other slides.

When you need to duplicate a slide, follow these steps:

1. Click the thumbnail-sized slide in the left pane.

2. Click the Home menu option, if necessary.

3. In the Slides section in the Home ribbon, click New Slide. (If the PowerPoint window has a small width, click Slides in the ribbon and then select New Slide from the drop-down menu.)

4. Select Duplicate Selected Slides from the drop-down menu, as shown in Figure 2.11.

FIGURE 2.11   The Duplicate Selected Slides option

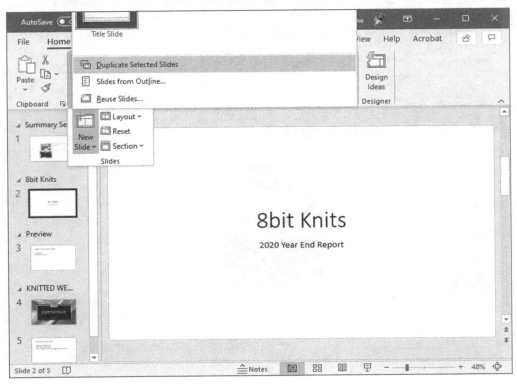

The duplicated slide is selected underneath the original slide in the list, and the duplicated slide appears in the right pane so that you can edit it.

When you want to select multiple slides to duplicate, you can do so in one of two ways. One is to select a contiguous group of slides by clicking on the first slide in the left pane, pressing and holding the Shift key, and then clicking the last slide in the pane. After you click Duplicate Selected Slides, as shown in step 4 earlier, the first selected slide, last selected slide, and all slides in between appear below the last selected slide.

You can also click the first slide in the left pane, press and hold the Ctrl key, and then click the slides that you want to duplicate. After you click Duplicate Selected Slides, as shown in step 4 earlier, the selected slides appear below the last slide in the slideshow regardless of whether the last slide has been selected.

EXERCISE 2.1

Inserting Slides

1. Open a new slideshow.

2. Add three slides with text in each one.

3. Insert a new slide after the second one and apply a layout to it.

4. Add a Summary Zoom slide for all four slides.

5. Replace the first slide in the Summary Zoom slide with a picture.

6. Duplicate slide 2 and slide 4.

7. Save the slideshow.

Modifying Slides

As you work on your slideshow, you may find that you need to modify your slides to make them look the way you want, as well as hide slides that don't apply to one or more of your audiences.

PowerPoint gives you the power to hide slides and show them again. You can also modify your slides by changing the background graphic and text, including the header, footer, and slide number, which PowerPoint calls a *page number*.

Hiding and Unhiding Slides

When you find that you need to hide slides during a presentation, such as those that discuss detailed financial information that are not of interest to the marketing department, you can hide slides. You can also tell PowerPoint to show those slides again when you want.

Here's how to hide a slide:

1. In the left pane, click the thumbnail-sized slide that you want to hide.

2. Click the Slide Show menu ribbon.

3. In the Set Up section in the Slide Show ribbon, click the Hide Slide icon.

In the left pane, the hidden slide appears with faded text and graphics and the slide number has a line through it (see Figure 2.12).

In the Slide Show ribbon, the Hide Slide icon is also in gray to show the slide is hidden. When you give your presentation and you show each slide, PowerPoint skips the hidden slide and moves to the next one.

FIGURE 2.12 The hidden slide in the left pane

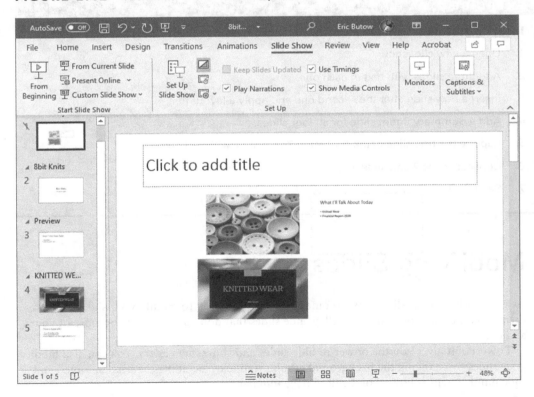

When you want to show the slide again, click the hidden slide in the left pane and then repeat steps 2 and 3. The gray shading in the slide disappears, and PowerPoint will show your slide during your presentation.

Showing a Hidden Slide During Your Presentation

If you find that you need to show a hidden slide as you give your presentation, such as in response to a question from the head of marketing about a specific line item on a financial slide that you hid, PowerPoint allows you to show a hidden slide within Presenter View as follows:

1. Click the Slide Show menu option if necessary.

2. In the Start Slide Show area in the Slide Show ribbon, click From Beginning.

3. When you see the first slide on the screen, right-click the screen.

4. Click Show All Slides in the pop-up menu.

5. In the list of thumbnail-sized slides, click the hidden slide that you want to show.

Now you can move to the next slide by clicking the down arrow or Page Down on your keyboard, or you can move to the previous slide by clicking the up arrow or Page Up on your keyboard.

Modifying Individual Slide Backgrounds

Though you can set backgrounds for your entire slideshow as you learned about in Chapter 1, you can also change a background for an individual slide. Here's how to do that:

1. Click the View menu option.

2. In the Presentation Views section in the View ribbon, click Normal (if necessary).

3. In the left pane, click the thumbnail-sized slide that you want to edit.

4. Click the Design menu option.

5. In the Customize section in the Design ribbon, click Format Background, as shown in Figure 2.13. (If the PowerPoint window has a small width, click Customize in the ribbon and then select Format Background from the drop-down menu.)

FIGURE 2.13   The Format Background option

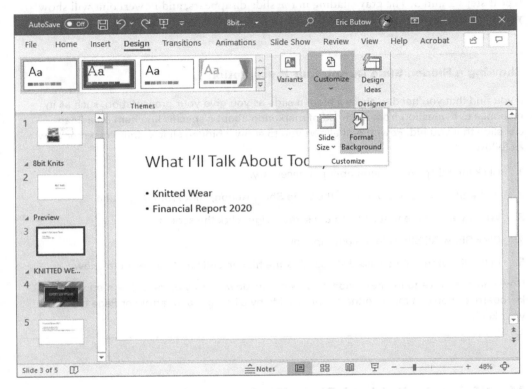

The Format Background pane appears on the right side of the PowerPoint window, as shown in Figure 2.14.

By default, the Solid Fill button is selected so that you can change the background fill color as well as the level of transparency from 0 percent (the default) to 100 percent, which means the color is invisible.

You can also click one of the three other buttons in the pane:

Gradient Fill: Set the color of the fill, the gradient type and direction, the gradient position, as well as the gradient transparency and brightness.

Picture or Texture Fill: Insert a picture or a textured background, change the transparency, and set the position of the picture or texture.

Pattern Fill: Select a pattern background from one of the 48 pattern swatches as well as the pattern foreground and background colors.

FIGURE 2.14   The Format Background pane

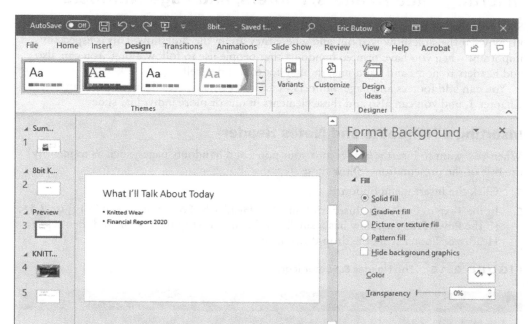

If you don't want to display graphics in the background, select the Hide Background Graphics check box.

As you make background changes, the slide changes so that you can see what each change looks like. If a change doesn't look good to you, press Ctrl+Z or click the Undo icon in the Quick Access Toolbar at the left side of the PowerPoint window title bar.

When you finish making changes, click the Close (X) icon in the upper-right corner of the Format Background pane.

If you want to apply your changes to all slides, click the Apply To All button at the bottom of the Format Background pane. You can also delete all of your background changes and start again by clicking the Reset Background button at the bottom of the pane.

Inserting Slide Headers, Footers, and Page Numbers

Slide footers and page numbers are good features to add when you want to let your audience know what the slideshow is about and where they are in the slideshow. This is especially important when you have printed handouts that people use to follow along. You can also add headers to notes and handouts, though not to a slide itself.

You can add footers and page numbers in a master slide, as you learned about in Chapter 1, and you can also add these elements in one or more individual slides.

Inserting a Handouts and Notes Header

When you want to insert a *header* into your notes and handouts pages, such as to identify the title of the presentation, follow these steps:

1. Click the Insert menu option.

2. In the Text section in the Insert ribbon, click Header & Footer, as shown in Figure 2.15. (If the PowerPoint window has a small width, click Text in the ribbon and then select Header & Footer from the drop-down menu.)

FIGURE 2.15 The Header & Footer icon

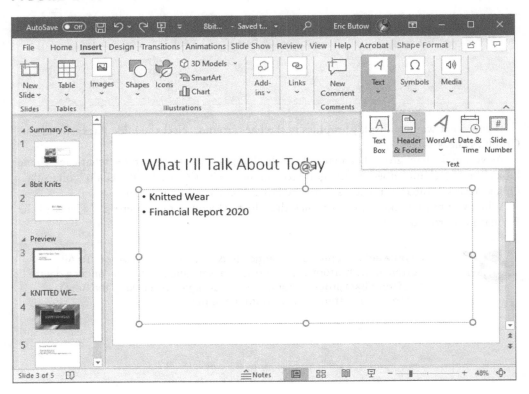

3. In the Header And Footer dialog box (see Figure 2.16), click the Notes And Handouts tab.

FIGURE 2.16   The Notes And Handouts tab

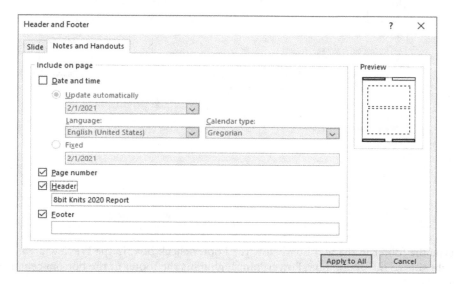

4. Select the Header check box. In the Preview area on the right side of the dialog box, PowerPoint highlights the header in the upper-left corner of the page.

5. Type the header in the text box below the Header check box.

6. Click Apply To All.

The dialog box closes, but you see no changes in any slide. You must print notes or handouts to display the header on the page.

Inserting a Slide Footer

Follow these steps to insert a *footer* into one or more slides:

1. Click the Insert menu option.

2. In the Text section in the Insert ribbon, click Header & Footer. (If the PowerPoint window has a small width, click Text in the ribbon and then select Header & Footer from the drop-down menu.)

3. In the Header And Footer dialog box, shown in Figure 2.17, select the Footer check box.

FIGURE 2.17   The Footer check box

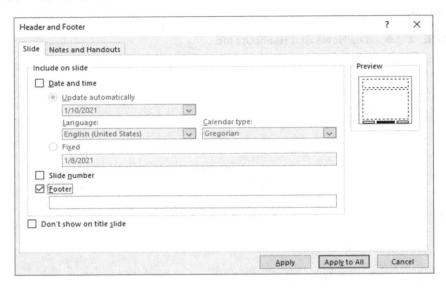

4. Type the footer in the text box below the Footer check box. In the Preview area on the right side of the dialog box, PowerPoint highlights the footer at the bottom center of the slide.

5. Click Apply to All to apply the footer to all slides.

There is more that you can do with a slide footer by selecting one or more of the following check boxes:

Date And Time   Add the current date and/or time. You can either have PowerPoint update this information every time you save the slideshow, or you can have a fixed date. In the Preview area, the footer on the left side of the slide appears so that you see where the date and time will be placed.

Slide Number   Add the page number to the slide, which you will learn how to do in the next section.

Don't Show On Title Slide   Don't show any footer information on the title slide.

Click Apply To All to apply the footer to all slides. If you have the Don't Show On Title Slide check box selected, then the footer will appear on all slides except the title slide.

Inserting a Page Number

PowerPoint includes all slides, including hidden slides, in the slide count. You can add the *page number* at the bottom of each slide as follows:

1. Click the Insert menu option.

2. In the Text section in the Insert ribbon, click Header & Footer. (If the PowerPoint window has a small width, click Text in the ribbon and then select Header & Footer from the drop-down menu.)

3. In the Header And Footer dialog box, shown in Figure 2.18, select the Slide Number check box.

FIGURE 2.18   The Slide Number check box

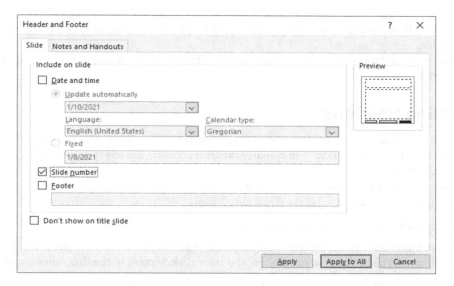

In the Preview area on the right side of the dialog box, PowerPoint highlights the header in the lower-right corner of the page.

Click Apply to apply the slide number to the current slide. Click Apply To All to apply the slide numbers to all slides.

EXERCISE 2.2

Modifying Slides

1. Open the slideshow that you created in Exercise 2.1.

2. Hide one of the slides, but not the Summary Zoom slide.

3. Apply a different background color to another slide.

4. Insert a slide number for all slides except the title slide.

5. Unhide the hidden slide.

6. Save the slideshow.

Ordering and Grouping Slides

As you create more slides, you may find that it becomes unwieldy to manage all of those slides. PowerPoint makes the process easier by providing tools to order and group your slides.

You can place your slides into sections, modify the order of slides, and rename your sections easily.

Creating Sections

Earlier in this chapter, you learned how PowerPoint automatically creates sections when you create a Summary Zoom slide. You can also create a *section* yourself to group slides in different categories.

Create a section by following these steps:

1. Click the slide where you want to insert a section.

2. Click the Home menu option, if necessary.

3. In the Slides section in the Home ribbon, click Section. (If the PowerPoint window has a small width, click Slides in the ribbon and then click Section in the drop-down menu.)

4. From the drop-down menu shown in Figure 2.19, select Add Section.

5. In the Rename Section dialog box, as shown in Figure 2.20, press Backspace to delete the default section name in the Section Name box and then type the new name.

FIGURE 2.19   The Add Section option

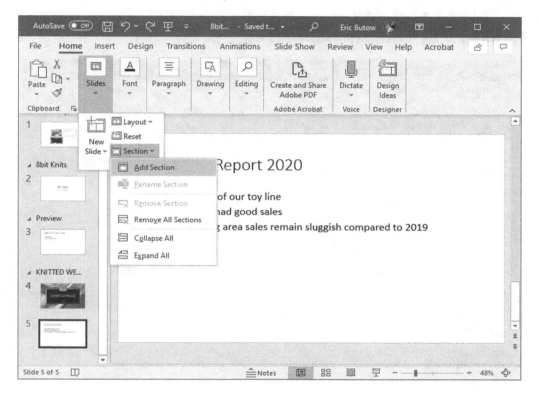

FIGURE 2.20   Rename Section dialog box

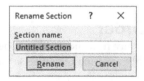

6. Click Rename. In the left pane, the slide is now contained within the section that has the new name (see Figure 2.21).

FIGURE 2.21   The section title above the slide

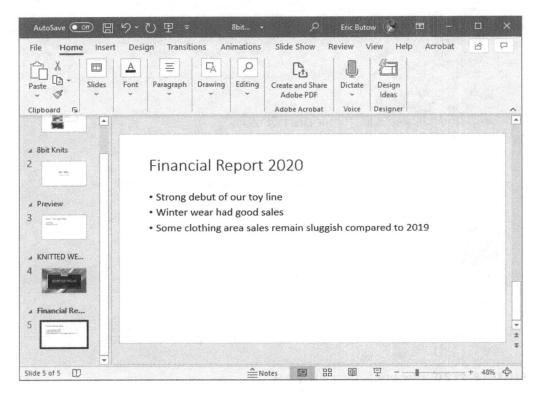

Modifying the Slide Order

As you create your slideshow, you may find the need to modify the order of slides so that your slideshow flows more smoothly (and makes more sense to your audience). You can also move a section that contains one or more slides.

Modify an Individual Slide

Modify the order of individual slides by following these steps:

1. Click the View menu option.
2. In the Presentation Views section in the View ribbon, click Normal (if necessary).
3. In the left pane, click and hold on the thumbnail-sized slide you want to edit.
4. Drag the slide up and down until the slide is where you want it.
5. When the slide is in your desired location, release the mouse button.

As you drag the selected slide in between other slides, the other slides move aside to make room for the slide you're moving.

 You can move multiple slides by pressing and holding the Ctrl key, clicking multiple slides in the left pane, and then clicking and dragging the slides to the new location.

Move a Section

When you want to move an entire section to another location, follow these steps:

1. Click the View menu option.
2. In the Presentation Views section in the View ribbon, click Normal (if necessary).
3. In the left pane, click and hold on the section title.
4. Drag the section title and move the sections up and down. All the slides disappear, and you only see the slide titles (see Figure 2.22).
5. When the section is where you want it, release the mouse button.

FIGURE 2.22   The selected slide in the left pane

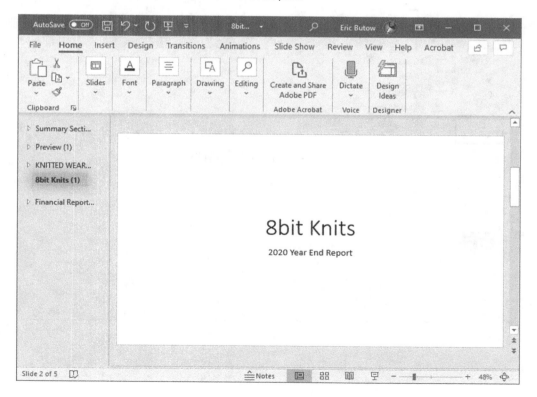

After you release the mouse button, the slides reappear. PowerPoint highlights the section title and the first slide within the section.

Renaming Sections

As you move slides and sections around, you may decide that a different section name better describes the slides within that section. You can rename a section by following these steps:

1. Click the Home menu option, if necessary.

2. In the left pane, click the section name you want to rename.

3. In the Slides section in the Home menu ribbon, click Section. (If the PowerPoint window has a small width, click Slides in the ribbon and then select Section from the drop-down menu.)

4. Select Rename Section from the drop-down menu, as shown in Figure 2.23.

FIGURE 2.23 Rename Section option

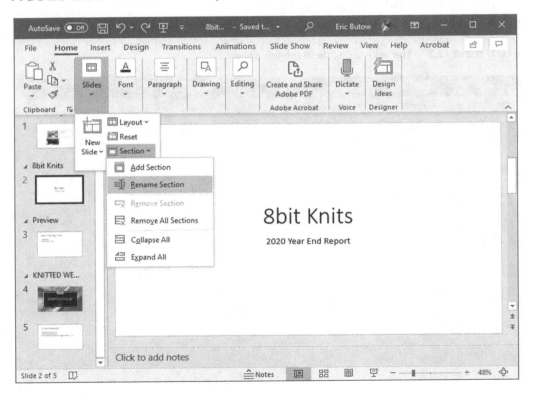

5. In the Rename Section dialog box (see Figure 2.24), press Backspace to delete the old
    section name in the Section Name text box.

FIGURE 2.24   Rename Section dialog box

6. Type the new name in the text box.
7. Click Rename.

    The selected section name shows your new name.

EXERCISE 2.3

Ordering and Grouping Slides

1. Open the slideshow that you created in Exercise 2.1.
2. Click the last slide (slide 4) in the slideshow.
3. Add a new slide (slide 5), as you learned to do earlier in this chapter.
4. Create a new section for slide 5.
5. Move one slide from one location to another.
6. Change the section name for slide 5.
7. Save the slideshow.

Summary

I started this chapter by showing you how to add slides from other files, including Word
document outlines and slides from another PowerPoint slideshow. Then you learned how to
insert slides from within your slideshow in PowerPoint and select a slide layout. Next you
learned how to insert Summary Zoom slides. You also learned how to duplicate one or more
slides.

Next, you saw how to hide and unhide slides within a slideshow. Then you learned about modifying individual slide backgrounds and inserting master slide backgrounds, which I discussed in Chapter 1. You also learned how to insert slide headers, footers, and page numbers.

You further learned about applying styles that Word provides automatically in new documents, which builds on what I discussed in Chapter 1. I finished that section by telling you how to clear all your formatting and start fresh without losing your text (and your time).

Finally, you learned how to order and group slides. I talked a bit about these tasks in Chapter 1. In this chapter, however, you learned much more, including how to create sections, modify the slide order in a slideshow, and rename sections.

Key Terms

headers	sections
footers	Summary Zoom

Exam Essentials

Understand how to import outlines.   Know how to import outlines created in Microsoft Word for use in creating a PowerPoint slideshow.

Understand how to import slides from another slideshow.   Know how to import slides from an existing PowerPoint slideshow into the open slideshow.

Understand how to insert slides and backgrounds.   Understand how to insert individual slides and set backgrounds for one or all slides in your slideshow.

Know how to insert Summary Zoom slides.   Understand what a Summary Zoom slide is, how to insert a Summary Zoom slide into your slideshow, and how to add one or more slides to the Summary Zoom slide.

Be able to duplicate slides.   Know how to duplicate one or more slides and place the slide(s) at another point within the slideshow.

Know how to modify slides.   Understand how to hide and unhide slides, set and change individual slide backgrounds, insert slide headers and footers, and place page numbers into one or all slides.

Understand how to order and group slides.   Know how to modify the order of slides in a slideshow as well as create and rename sections.

Review Questions

1. When you add more pages of an outline than will fit on a slide, what happens?

   A. A dialog box appears telling you that the outline was too long.

   B. You only see the outline text that fits in the slide.

   C. PowerPoint creates additional slides to accommodate the text.

   D. A dialog box appears that says PowerPoint cannot add the outline because it's too long.

2. How do you know a slide is hidden in the list of slides in the left pane?

   A. The slide no longer exists in the list.

   B. The hidden slide appears with a gray background, and the slide number has a line through it.

   C. The hidden slide number has a line through it, but the slide no longer exists in the list.

   D. Click Slide Sorter in the View ribbon.

3. When you create a section, what option do you click in the Slides drop-down menu?

   A. Section and then click Remove Sections

   B. Layout and then click Blank Slide

   C. New Slide and then click Section Header

   D. Section and then click Add Section

4. How do you keep the formatting contained in an imported slide when you import it into your slideshow?

   A. After you import the slide, a dialog box asks you if you want to keep the formatting when you import it.

   B. Right-click the imported slide in the Reuse Slides pane and then click Keep Source Formatting in the menu.

   C. Select the Keep Source Formatting check box in the Reuse Slides pane.

   D. Click Browse in the Reuse Slides pane and then select the correct file type in the Browse dialog box.

5. What other types of fills can you add to a slide background? (Choose all that apply.)

   A. Gradient fill

   B. Solid fill

   C. Pattern fill

   D. Hide background graphics

6. What key do you press and hold to select more than one slide to move?

   A. Ins

   B. Alt

    C. Shift

    D. Ctrl

7. When you click a slide in the list of slides in Normal view, where does a new slide appear?

    A. Above the selected slide

    B. Below the selected slide

    C. As the first slide in the slideshow

    D. As the last slide in the slideshow

8. Where does a page number appear in a slide?

    A. Bottom-right corner

    B. Bottom-left corner

    C. Bottom and centered

    D. Top-right corner

9. What menu option do you click to rename a section?

    A. Design

    B. Insert

    C. Home

    D. Review

10. How many slides does PowerPoint add to a Summary Zoom slide?

    A. All the slides

    B. The first three

    C. You can choose the slides you want to add in a dialog box that appears after you create the Summary Zoom slide.

    D. One slide per section

Chapter 3

Inserting and Formatting Text, Shapes, and Images

MICROSOFT EXAM OBJECTIVES COVERED IN THIS CHAPTER:

✓ **Insert and format text, shapes, and images**

- Format text
  - Apply formatting and styles to text
  - Format text in multiple columns
  - Create bulleted and numbered lists
- Insert links
  - Insert hyperlinks
  - Insert Section Zoom links and Slide Zoom links
- Insert and format images
  - Resize and crop images
  - Apply built-in styles and effects to images
  - Insert screenshots and screen clippings
- Insert and format graphic elements
  - Insert and change shapes
  - Draw by using digital ink
  - Add text to shapes and text boxes
  - Resize shapes and text boxes
  - Format shapes and text boxes
  - Apply built-in styles to shapes and text boxes
  - Add Alt text to graphic elements for accessibility

- Order and group objects on slides
  - Order shapes, images, and text boxes
  - Align shapes, images, and text boxes
  - Group shapes and images
  - Display alignment tools

PowerPoint gives you the ability to communicate your message effectively using both text and graphics in your slides. After you place your text and/or graphics in your slideshow, you can use the built-in formatting tools to make the text and graphics look the way you want.

This chapter starts by showing you how to add and format text in slides that will help you communicate your message with various styles, columns, and lists. You can also add hyperlinks to external sources, such as websites, and insert links to Section Zoom and Slide Zoom slides.

Next, I'll show you how to insert images, either from your own computer or from stock libraries installed with PowerPoint. After you add an image, you can resize it, add styles, and apply effects. What's more, you can add screenshots of your computer and place screen clippings, which are a portion of your screen, into your slideshow.

I also talk about adding and formatting shapes and images, adding text boxes, adding text to graphic elements, and positioning those images so that they look good on the page. You will also learn how to add alternative, or Alt, text to images and photos so that people who cannot see them can read a description.

Finally, you will learn how to order your text boxes, shapes, and images to place them where you want on one or more slides.

Formatting Text

PowerPoint makes it easy to add text to a Slide Master or an individual slide and then format the style the way you want. That can include things as basic as changing the font from normal to bold, or you can apply built-in styles to make your text pop.

You can also format your text in ways that are similar to Microsoft Word, including laying out the text in multiple columns, bulleted lists, or numbered lists.

Applying Formatting and Styles to Text

PowerPoint has several tools at the ready so that you can apply formatting and styles to your text. These include the Format Painter, the ability to set line and paragraph spacing, the ability to indent a paragraph, and built-in styles. You can also clear formatting that you've made at any time.

Applying Formatting by Using Format Painter

The *Format Painter* feature is a quick and easy way to apply formatting from selected text or an entire paragraph to another block of text or a paragraph. Follow these steps to get started:

1. Select the text or click text in a slide that has the formatting you want to copy.

2. Click the Home menu option if it's not selected already.

3. In the Home ribbon, click the Format Painter icon in the Clipboard area, as shown in Figure 3.1.

FIGURE 3.1 Format Painter icon

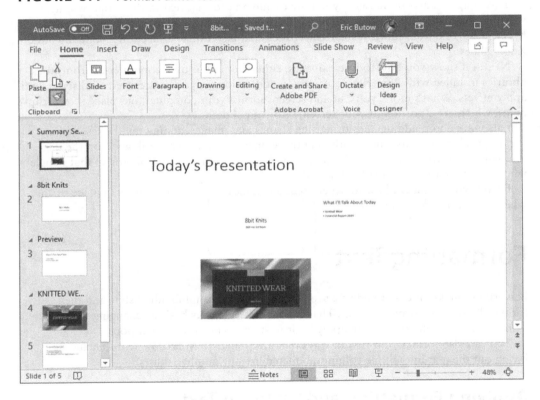

The mouse pointer changes to a cursor icon combined with a paintbrush. Now you can select a block of text or click inside a paragraph. The text or paragraph that you selected now shows the format that you copied.

This process works only once, but you can change the format of multiple blocks of text or paragraphs. After you select the text with the formatting that you want to copy, double-click the Format Painter icon in the Home toolbar and then select the text and/or paragraphs. When you're done, press the Esc key.

Setting Line Spacing

You may need to change spacing between lines so that your audience has no trouble reading the text on your slide. When you want to set line spacing, place the cursor where you want to start the different line spacing, or select the text that will have the different line spacing. In the Home ribbon, click the Line Spacing icon in the Paragraph area. (If your PowerPoint window width is small, click the Paragraph icon and then click the Line Spacing icon.)

Now you can select one of the built-in line spacing amounts, as shown in Figure 3.2. For example, selecting 2.0 means that you will see double-spaced lines as you type.

FIGURE 3.2   Line Spacing drop-down menu

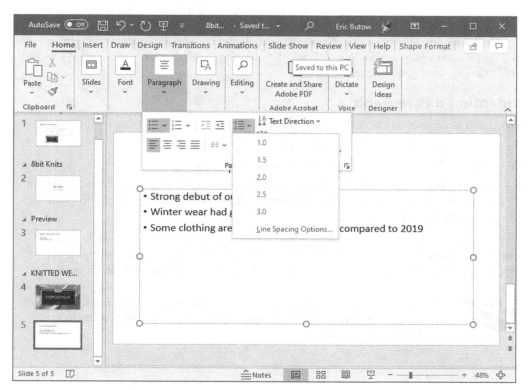

Below the list of built-in line spacing amounts, select Line Spacing Options to open the Paragraph dialog box (see Figure 3.3) to change specific line spacing settings.

FIGURE 3.3   Paragraph dialog box

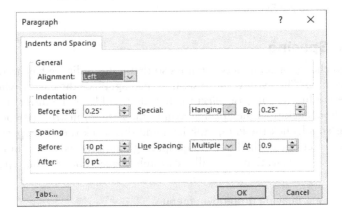

The dialog box allows you to change the text alignment, specific indentation settings, and specific line spacing. (If you use Word, these settings probably look familiar.) When you finish making changes, click OK.

Indenting a Paragraph

When you need to indent text, follow these steps:

1. Place the cursor in the text that you want to change.
2. Click the Home menu option if it's not selected already.
3. In the Home ribbon, click the Increase List Level icon in the Paragraph area, as shown in Figure 3.4. (If your PowerPoint window width is small, click the Paragraph icon and then click the Line Spacing icon.)

PowerPoint indents the text by 0.5 inches. Whenever you click the Increase List Level icon, PowerPoint increases the indent by an additional 0.5 inches. You can decrease the indent by 0.5 inches by clicking the Decrease List Level icon that you saw in Figure 3.4.

If you indent a bullet or numbered list, the line reflects the formatting for the next list level. If you decrease the indent, the line reflects the formatting for the previous list level.

FIGURE 3.4   Decrease List Level (left) and Increase List Level (right) icons

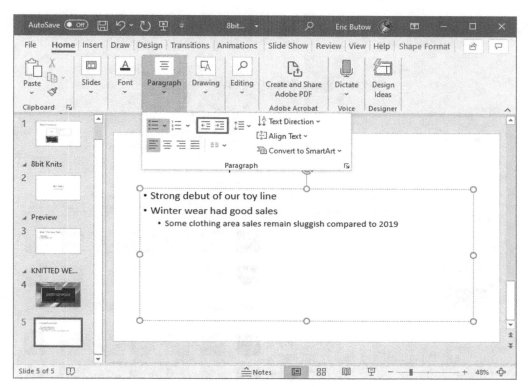

Applying Built-In Styles to Text

When you open a new document, PowerPoint includes 77 different styles for you to apply to text. You can view and apply these styles to text by clicking the Home menu option if it's not already active.

In the Drawing area in the Home ribbon, click Quick Styles in the ribbon, as shown in Figure 3.5. (If your PowerPoint window width is small, click the Drawing icon and then click Quick Styles.)

As you move the mouse pointer over each style, the slide area that contains the text changes to reflect the style. When you find a style that you like, click the style in the drop-down menu. PowerPoint closes the drop-down menu so that you can see the slide with the style applied to the slide area.

FIGURE 3.5   The Quick Styles drop-down menu

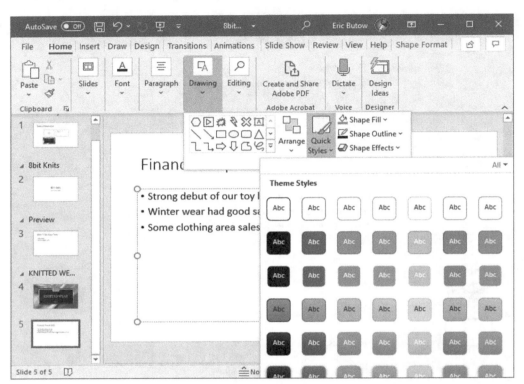

 If you want a different background for the slide area, move the mouse pointer over Other Theme Fills at the bottom of the drop-down menu, and then move the mouse pointer over one of the 12 background color tiles to see how each color will look in the slide area. If you like one, select the tile to close the drop-down menu.

Clearing Formatting

You can clear formatting in selected text by clicking the Home menu option (if necessary). In the Font area in the Home ribbon, click the Clear All Formatting icon, as shown in Figure 3.6. (If your PowerPoint window width is small, click the Font icon and then click the Clear All Formatting icon.)

The text reverts to the default Normal paragraph style. However, if this text has other paragraph formatting—for example, it's in a bulleted or numbered list—the paragraph formatting remains intact.

FIGURE 3.6   Clear All Formatting icon

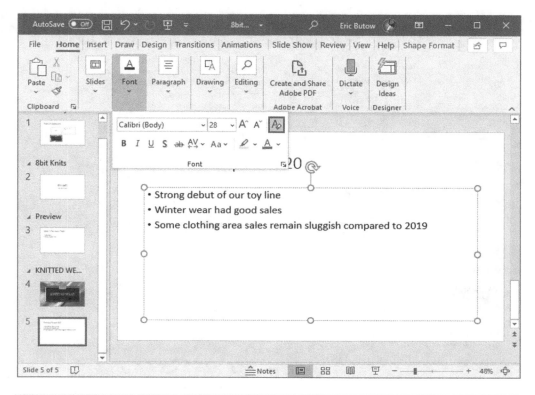

> **NOTE**
>
> What if you want to clear the formatting of all the text in a slide area?
> Press Ctrl+A to select all the text and then click Clear All Formatting in the
> Font section in the Home ribbon.

Formatting Text in Multiple Columns

If you want to put text into more than one column on a slide to make it easier to read, here
are the steps to add multiple columns in a PowerPoint slide:

1. In the slide area that contains the text, click anywhere in the text.

2. Click the Home menu option, if necessary.

3. In the Paragraph section in the Home ribbon, click the Add Or Remove Columns icon.
    (If your PowerPoint window width is small, click the Paragraph icon and then click the
    Line Spacing icon.)

4. Select the number of columns from the drop-down list (see Figure 3.7). The default is
    One. You can select as many as Three.

FIGURE 3.7   Add Or Remove Columns menu

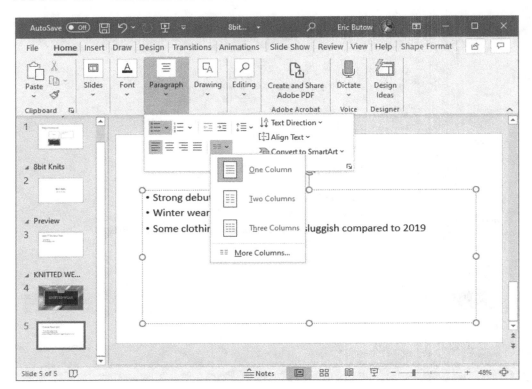

If you want even more control over your columns, click More Columns in the drop-down list. The Columns dialog box appears so that you can change the number of columns and the spacing between each column.

Creating Bulleted and Numbered Lists

An entry in a list, whether it's a few words or a few sentences, is treated as a paragraph. PowerPoint makes it easy to change a paragraph to a numbered list or a bulleted list.

Create a List

You don't need to do anything special to create a numbered or bulleted list.

Start a numbered list by typing **1**, a period (.), a space, and then your text. When you finish typing your text, press Enter. PowerPoint formats the first entry in your list and places you on the next line in the numbered list with the number 2.

Create a bulleted list by typing an asterisk (*), a space, and then your text. When you're done typing, press Enter. The asterisk changes to a black circle and places you on the next line with another black circle to the left so that you can continue working on your list.

You can also start a numbered or bulleted list from within the Home ribbon. If you don't see it, click the Home menu option. In the ribbon, click the Bullets or the Numbering icon in the Paragraph section, as shown in Figure 3.8. (If your PowerPoint window width is small, click the Paragraph icon and then click the Bullets or Numbering icon.)

FIGURE 3.8   Bullets (left) and Numbering (right) icons

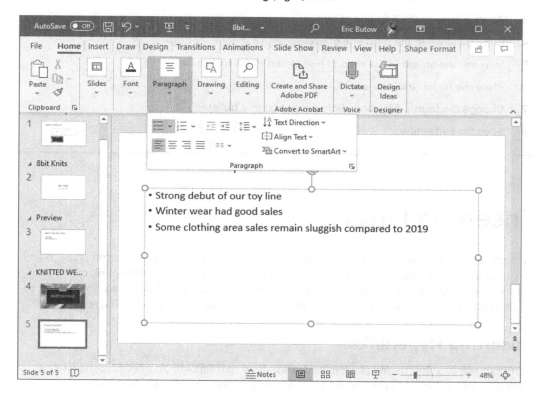

Now you see the number 1 or a bullet circle to the left of your cursor, and you can start typing your list. When you reach the last item in your list, press Enter twice to switch the bullets or numbering off.

Create a List from Existing Text

Using the Home ribbon, you can easily create a list from text you've already written. Start by selecting the text you want to convert to a list, and then click the Bullets or Numbering icon in the Paragraph section. Each paragraph in the text appears as a separate number or bullet in the list.

You can continue the list by clicking the last item in the list and then pressing Enter. If the list is fine as is, click outside the selection.

EXERCISE 3.1

Formatting Text

1. Create a new slideshow.

2. In the first slide, type six lines of text.

3. Apply a style to the first line of text.

4. Copy the style to the third line of text.

5. Increase the indent in the second line of text to 0.5 inches.

6. Place the text in three columns.

7. Change the fourth, fifth, and sixth line of text to a bulleted list.

8. Save the slideshow.

Inserting Links

PowerPoint allows you to add a hyperlink to your document, such as when you want to link to an external web page that you want your audience to see. If you want to link to the Summary Zoom page that you learned about in Chapter 2, "Managing Slides," or if you want to link to selected slides, you can link to Summary Zoom and Slide Zoom pages, respectively.

Inserting Hyperlinks

You can put in a link in one place in your slideshow that links to another place, such as a link on Slide 3 that will take you to the slide that contains the list of topics covered in your presentation.

Here's how to add a link:

1. Click the text in the slide that you want to use in the link.

2. Click the Insert menu option.

3. In the Links section in the Insert ribbon, click the Link icon. (If your PowerPoint window width is small, click the Links icon and then click the Link icon.)

4. Select Insert Link from the drop-down menu.

5. In the Insert Hyperlink dialog box, shown in Figure 3.9, click the Place In This Document option under Link To.

FIGURE 3.9   Insert Hyperlink dialog box

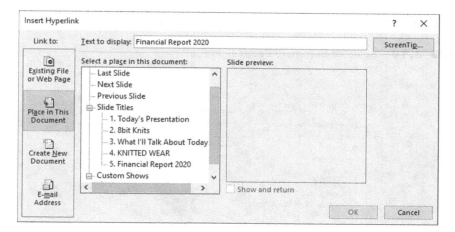

6. Click what you want to link to. In this example, click Financial Report 2020 in the Select A Place In This Document list box.

7. Click OK.

The link in the text is blue with an underline. When you run your slideshow and click the link, the linked slide appears on the screen.

Inserting Section Zoom Links and Slide Zoom Links

When you create a Section Zoom or Slide Zoom, you can link to those zoom slides easily. Although Chapter 2 didn't cover adding a Slide Zoom, I will show you how to create a new Slide Zoom in this section and then link to it.

Linking to a Summary Zoom Slide

Link to a *Summary Zoom* slide by following these steps:

1. Click the text in the slide that you want to use in the link.

2. Click the Insert menu option.

3. In the Links section in the Insert ribbon, click the Link icon. (If your PowerPoint window width is small, click the Links icon and then click the Link icon.)

4. Select Insert Link from the drop-down menu.

5. In the Insert Hyperlink dialog box, click the Place In This Document option under Link To.

6. Select the Summary Zoom slide you want to link to, which is the first slide in this example. The Summary Zoom slide has only the name of the slide, which is Slide 1 (see Figure 3.10).

7. Click OK.

FIGURE 3.10 Selected Summary Zoom slide

The link in the text is blue and underlined. When you run your slideshow and click the link, the Summary Zoom slide appears on the screen.

Creating a Slide Zoom Slide

A *Slide Zoom* is good to use when you have a small slideshow so you can have links to all of your slides from within the Slide Zoom slide. Before you can link to a slide with a Slide Zoom, you need to create the Slide Zoom first. Here's how to do that:

1. Click the slide below which the Slide Zoom slide will appear.

2. Click the Insert menu option.

3. In the Slides section in the Insert ribbon, click New Slide.

4. Select the Blank thumbnail-sized slide template from the drop-down list.

5. In the Links section in the Insert ribbon, click the Zoom icon. (If your PowerPoint window width is small, click the Links icon and then click the Zoom icon.)

6. Select Slide Zoom from the drop-down menu.

7. In the Insert Slide Zoom dialog box, shown in Figure 3.11, click the thumbnail-sized slide(s) that you want to include in the Slide Zoom slide.

8. Click Insert.

FIGURE 3.11   Insert Slide Zoom dialog box

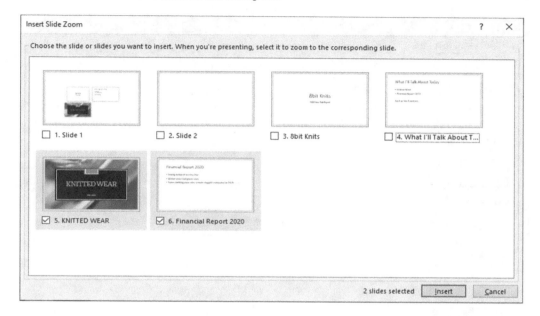

Thumbnail-sized slides appear within the slide (see Figure 3.12) tiled one atop another. You can move slides around by clicking the part of the slide that you want to move and then clicking and dragging the slide to a new location on the parent slide.

 When you click one of the thumbnail-sized slides in the Slide Zoom slide, sizing handles appear around the slide so that you can click one of the handles and drag the handle to resize the slide within the parent slide.

Linking to a Slide Zoom Slide

Now that you have created a Slide Zoom slide, you can link to it from another slide. The process is similar to linking to a Summary Zoom slide:

1. Click the text in the slide that you want to use in the link.

2. Click the Insert menu option.

3. In the Links section in the Insert ribbon, click the Link icon. (If your PowerPoint window width is small, click the Links icon and then click the Link icon.)

4. Select Insert Link from the drop-down menu.

5. In the Insert Hyperlink dialog box, click the Place In This Document option under Link To.

FIGURE 3.12   Thumbnail-sized slides within the Slide Zoom

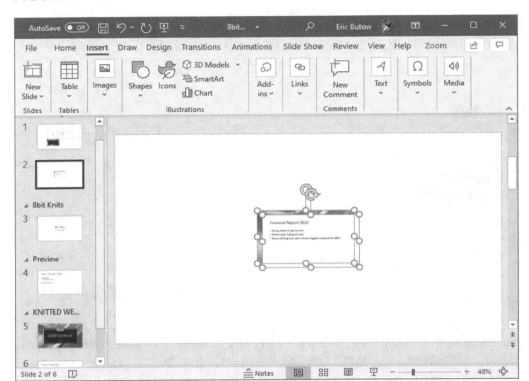

6. Select the Slide Zoom slide you want to link to, which is the second slide in this example. The Slide Zoom slide has only the name of the slide, which is Slide 2 (see Figure 3.13).

7. Click OK.

FIGURE 3.13   Selected Slide Zoom slide

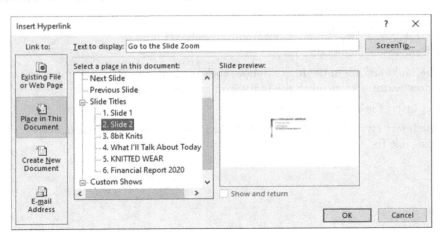

Like other text links, the link text is blue and underlined. When you run your slideshow and click the link, the Slide Zoom slide appears on the screen.

EXERCISE 3.2

Inserting Links

1. Open the slideshow that you created in Exercise 3.1.

2. In Slide 4, add text (if necessary) and then add a hyperlink to Slide 1 in the text.

3. Create a Slide Zoom slide after Slide 1 in the slideshow.

4. In Slide 5, add text (if necessary) and then add a hyperlink to the Slide Zoom slide in the text.

5. Save the slideshow.

Inserting and Formatting Images

PowerPoint makes it easy to add images, apply styles and effects to those images, as well as add screenshots and clippings of your screen into a slide so that you don't have to switch back and forth between your presentation and another window or your Windows desktop.

You can add pictures stored on your computer, stock images that were installed with PowerPoint, or pictures available on the http://office.com website. Here's how:

1. In the slide, place your cursor where you want to insert the image.

2. Click the Insert menu option.

3. In the Insert ribbon, click Pictures in the Images section. (If your PowerPoint window width is small, click the Images icon and then click Pictures.)

4. From the drop-down menu, shown in Figure 3.14, select one of the following options:

   This Device: Click this option to browse for and select a photo from your computer.

   Stock Images: Click this option to view and open a stock image on your computer.

   Online Pictures: Click this option to view and open an image from Office.com.

   For this example, I'll open a stock image. By default, the Images dialog box opens with the stock images displayed selected, as shown in Figure 3.15.

5. Scroll up and down in the list of thumbnail images until you find the one that you want, and then click the image.

6. Click Insert.

FIGURE 3.14   Pictures drop-down menu

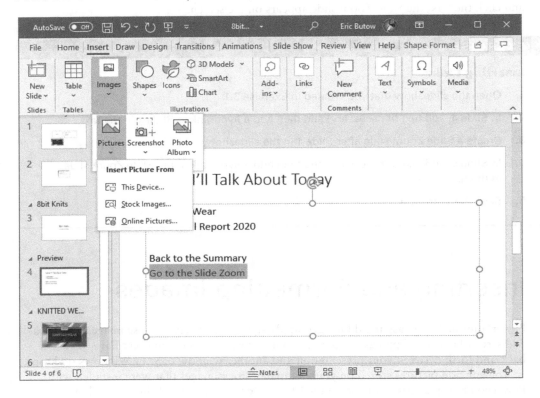

FIGURE 3.15   Images dialog box

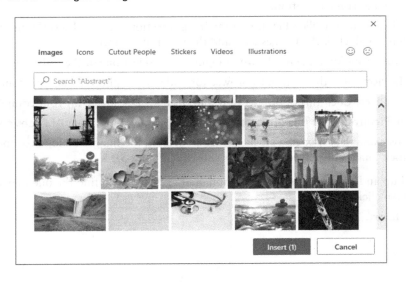

The image appears in the document, and text moves underneath the image. You'll learn how to move the image and change the text wrapping style later in this chapter.

Resizing and Cropping Images

If an inserted image is smaller than the size of the slide, then PowerPoint places the entire image in the center of the slide. If the image is larger than the size of the slide, PowerPoint automatically resizes the image so that the height of the image is the same as the slide height.

PowerPoint makes it easy to resize images in a slide. When you want to crop an image to focus on a specific area of an image, you can crop an image to remove many of the features that you find extraneous.

Resize an Image

Once you click an image, you have two ways to resize it:

- Click and drag one of the sizing handles to change the width or height. If you want to change both the width and height, then click and drag one of the corner sizing handles.

- In the Picture Format ribbon that appears after you click the image, type the height and width in the Shape Height and Shape Width boxes, respectively, in the Size section (see Figure 3.16).

FIGURE 3.16   Shape Height (top) and Width (bottom) boxes

Crop an Image

Crop an image within a slide by following these steps:

1. Click the image in the slide.
2. In the Size section in the Picture Format ribbon, click Crop.
3. From the drop-down menu, shown in Figure 3.17, select Crop.

FIGURE 3.17   The Crop menu option

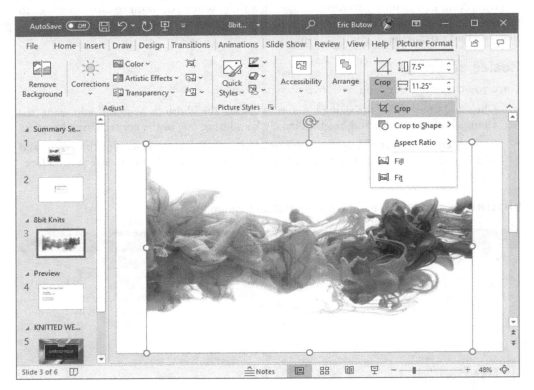

4. Click and hold the mouse button on one of the black resizing handles around the perimeter of the image.

    The cursor changes to a T- or L-shaped bar depending on the handle that you select.

5. Drag the mouse pointer until the cropped image appears the way that you want.

    As you drag, the image area that you are removing appears in dark gray.

6. When you're done, release the mouse button.

7. In the Size section in the Picture Format ribbon, click the Crop icon (see Figure 3.18).

    PowerPoint replaces the crop handles with sizing handles around the cropped image.

FIGURE 3.18   The Crop icon in the Picture Format ribbon

Applying Built-In Styles and Effects to Images

PowerPoint also allows you to set effects from within the Picture Format ribbon. However, if you don't need to have fine-tuned effects on your picture, PowerPoint has prebuilt styles for you that you can apply to the selected picture by clicking the appropriate tile in the ribbon.

Apply a Picture Style

Apply a *picture style* from the ribbon by following these steps:

1. Click the image in the slide.

2. In the Picture Styles section in the Picture Format ribbon, move the mouse pointer over the thumbnail-sized style tiles in the Picture Styles section, as shown in Figure 3.19. (If the PowerPoint window isn't very wide, click Quick Styles in the ribbon to view a drop-down ribbon with the style icons.)

   As you move the pointer over every style icon, the picture in your document changes to reflect the style.

3. Apply the style by clicking the icon.

FIGURE 3.19 Quick Styles style tiles

If you don't like any of the styles, move the icon away from the row of styles and the picture reverts to its default state.

Add a Picture Effect

Here's how to choose and add a *picture effect*:

1. Click the picture.

2. In the Picture Styles section in the Picture Format ribbon, click Picture Effects.

3. In the drop-down menu, move the mouse pointer to one of the seven effects that you want to add. I selected Shadow in this example.

4. In the side menu, move the mouse pointer over the tile that contains the shadow style. The style is applied to the picture in your slide so that you can see what it looks like (see Figure 3.20).

5. When you find an effect that you like, click the tile in the menu.

FIGURE 3.20   Offset: Center shadow style applied to the picture

If you want to change the effect, select Options from the bottom of the menu. For example, in Shadow, select Shadow Options. The Format Picture pane appears on the right side of the PowerPoint window so that you can make more detailed changes, such as the color of the shadow.

Inserting Screenshots and Screen Clippings

You can take a photo of another window and add it directly into your document from within PowerPoint. You can also clip a portion of your screen within PowerPoint and add it to your document automatically.

Screenshot

Add a *screenshot* to your document by following these steps:

1. Place your cursor where you want to insert the screenshot.
2. Click the Insert menu option.

3. In the Insert ribbon, click Screenshot in the Images section. (If your PowerPoint window width is small, click the Images icon and then click Screenshot.) If any windows are open, PowerPoint scans your computer and places thumbnail-sized images of the windows within the drop-down list, as shown in Figure 3.21.

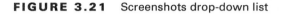

FIGURE 3.21 Screenshots drop-down list

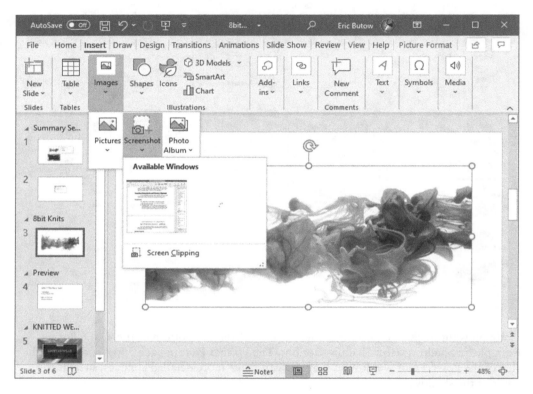

The currently open PowerPoint window is one of the windows that PowerPoint finds. When you click the window in the list, PowerPoint places the screenshot at the insertion point in your document.

Screen Clipping

You can clip the entire screen or a portion of it. Here's how to add a *screen clipping*:

1. Place your cursor where you want to insert the screenshot.

2. Click the Insert menu option.

3. In the Insert ribbon, click Screenshot in the Images section. (If your PowerPoint window width is small, click the Images icon and then click Screenshot.)

4. Select Screen Clipping from the drop-down list. PowerPoint automatically opens the last window that you had open prior to using PowerPoint. If you didn't have a window open, you see the desktop. The screen has a transparent white overlay, and the mouse pointer changes to a cross, which means that PowerPoint is ready for you to capture the screen.

5. Move the cursor to the location where you want to start capturing the screen.

6. Hold down the mouse button and drag until you've captured your selection (see Figure 3.22).

FIGURE 3.22   Capture area

7. Release the mouse button.

   The clipped image appears within the slide and the Design Ideas pane appears at the right side of the PowerPoint window so that you can view suggestions for placing the screen clipping and any other images within the slide. You can apply the suggested design by clicking the thumbnail image within the Design Ideas pane.

EXERCISE 3.3

Inserting and Formatting Images

1. Open the slideshow that you created in Exercise 3.1.

2. In Slide 1, add a new stock image.

3. Resize the image to a smaller size of your choosing in the slide.

4. Apply a picture style to the image.

5. Go to Slide 3.

6. Add a screenshot to the slide.

7. Save the slideshow.

Inserting and Formatting Graphic Elements

PowerPoint makes it easy to choose and insert shapes and text boxes, and even annotate your slides with handwriting, which is what PowerPoint calls *digital ink*.

After you add a shape, text box, or handwriting, PowerPoint gives you plenty of tools to format them to make them look the way you want and then place them where you want on the page. You can even convert a handwritten drawing into a shape.

Inserting and Changing Shapes

PowerPoint contains many built-in shapes that you can add to your document, from lines to callouts like the speech balloons that you find in graphic novels and comic strips. When you add a shape, you place the item on the slide and then size the shape to your needs.

Add a shape by following these steps:

1. Select the slide where you want to add the shape.

2. Click the Insert menu option.

3. In the Insert ribbon, click Shapes in the Illustrations section.

4. Select a shape icon from the drop-down list (see Figure 3.23). The mouse pointer changes from an arrow to a cross.

FIGURE 3.23   The shapes drop-down list

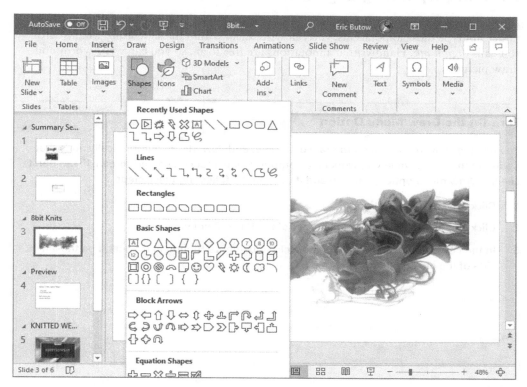

5. Move the pointer to the location in your slide where you want to add the shape.

6. Hold down the mouse button, and then drag the shape to the size you want.

7. When you're done, release the mouse button.

The shape appears in front of the text in the slide. You can resize the shape by clicking and dragging one of the sizing handles around the perimeter of the shape.

You can also add an *action button*, which is a button in your slide that performs a specific function when you click it. For example, when you insert the Play button, you can change what the Play button does.

Adding an action button is beyond the purview of the MO-300 exam, but you can still add one and see what it looks like by clicking and dragging one of the buttons from the action button section at the bottom of the shapes drop-down list that you saw in Figure 3.23.

Drawing by Using Digital Ink

If you ever need to annotate your slides in a presentation or in notes, and you would rather not type those annotations, you can write them within the slide using what Microsoft calls *digital ink*. Handwritten annotations are free form, so you can write words and draw pictures.

Turn On the Draw Menu Option

You use the Draw menu option to draw on a slide, and PowerPoint automatically adds that option to the menu when you work on a computer with a touch-enabled screen. If you don't see the Draw menu option, you can add it yourself by following these steps:

1. Click the File menu option.

2. Click Options at the bottom-left corner of the PowerPoint window.

3. In the PowerPoint Options dialog box, click Customize Ribbon in the menu on the left side of the dialog box.

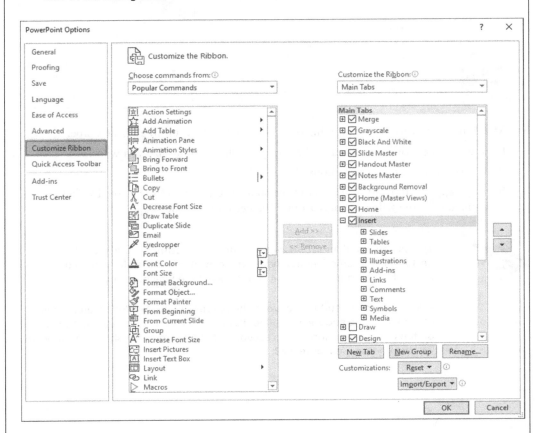

4. In the Customize The Ribbon list on the right side of the dialog box, select the Draw check box.

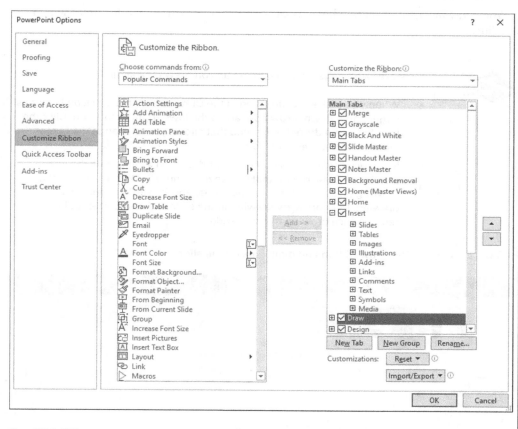

5. Click OK.

The Draw menu option appears between Insert and Design in the menu bar.

Draw on a slide using digital ink by following these steps:

1. Click the slide you want to draw on in the left pane.

2. Click the Draw menu option.

3. In the Drawing Tools section in the Draw ribbon, click one of the three drawing icons: Pen (Black), Pen (Red), or Highlighter.

4. Move the mouse pointer over the slide.

5. Click and hold on the spot where you want to start drawing, and then drag to draw.

6. When you're finished, release the mouse button.

Your drawing appears on the slide. Repeat steps 5 and 6 to draw in other areas within the slide.

Here are two things to keep in mind as you draw on a slide:

▪ When you click a drawing icon in the Draw ribbon, the pen icon becomes larger and a down arrow appears to the lower-right of the icon. Click the icon to open a drop-down menu that allows you to change the pen or highlighter thickness and color.

▪ If you want to erase anything you've drawn on a slide, click the Eraser icon in the Draw ribbon that you saw in Figure 3.24. Then click on the drawing (such as a not-so-straight line) and PowerPoint deletes that drawing. Click on every drawing in the slide with the Eraser tool to remove each drawing that you added.

FIGURE 3.24   The Draw ribbon and digital ink on the slide

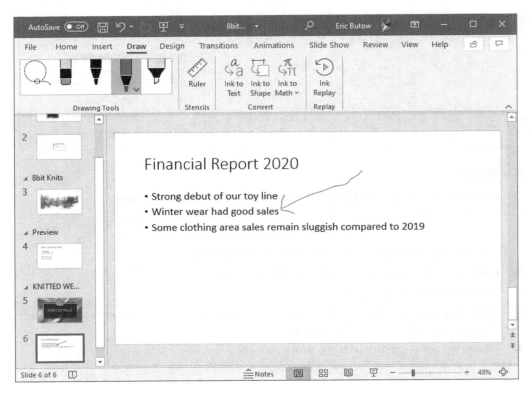

Adding Text to Shapes and Text Boxes

After you add a shape, PowerPoint gives you the ability to add text to a shape. And after you add a text box, PowerPoint makes it easy to add text within the box.

Add Text to a Shape

In a shape, start by right-clicking anywhere in your shape and then clicking Edit Text in the context menu, as shown in Figure 3.25.

FIGURE 3.25   Edit Text option

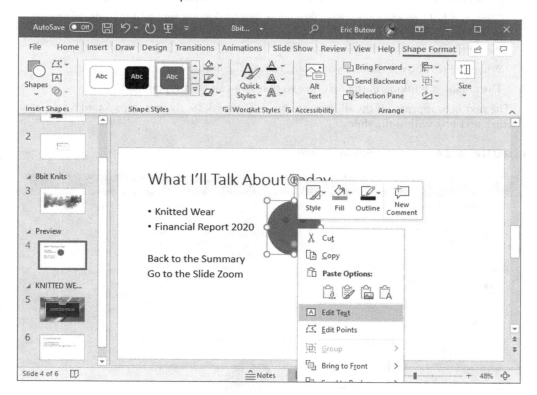

The cursor appears in the center of the shape so that you can type your text. When you finish typing, click outside the text box or the shape.

Add a Text Box

Before you can add text to a text box, you need to know how to add a text box first, so follow these steps:

1. In the left pane, click the slide in which you want to add the text box.

2. Click the Insert menu option.

3. In the Text section in the Insert ribbon, click Text Box. (If your PowerPoint window width is small, click the Text icon and then click Text Box.)

4. Move the mouse pointer over the slide. The cursor changes to a straight line with a small perpendicular line near the bottom, which makes the cursor look like a little sword.

5. Click and hold on the spot where you want to add the text box and then drag the mouse. As you drag, the cursor changes to a cross and you see the boundary of the text box.

6. When the text box is the size you want, release the mouse button.

7. The cursor is blinking in the text box so that you can start typing text.

The text box appears on the slide, as shown in Figure 3.26. Repeat steps 5 and 6 to create another text box within the slide.

FIGURE 3.26 The text box in the slide

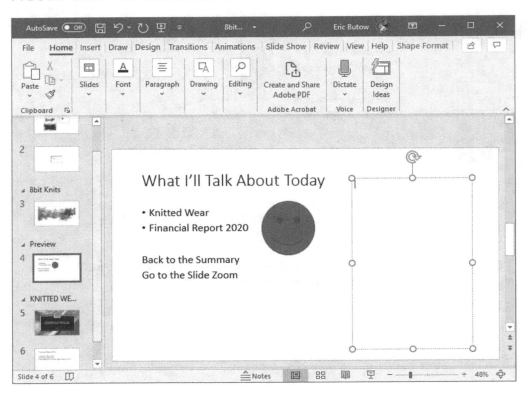

Resizing Shapes and Text Boxes

PowerPoint makes it easy to resize shapes and text boxes. You can do so in one of two ways: clicking and dragging one of the handles around the boundary of the shape or text box, or changing the size in the Shape Format ribbon.

Resize a Shape

All you need to do to resize a shape manually is to click the shape, click and hold one sizing handle around the boundary of the shape, and then drag the shape until it's the size you want.

If you want to set the exact height and/or width of the shape, type the measurement in inches in the Height and/or Width boxes in the Size section in the Shape Format ribbon, as shown in Figure 3.27. (If your PowerPoint window width is small, click the Size icon and then type the height and/or width.)

FIGURE 3.27   Height and Width boxes

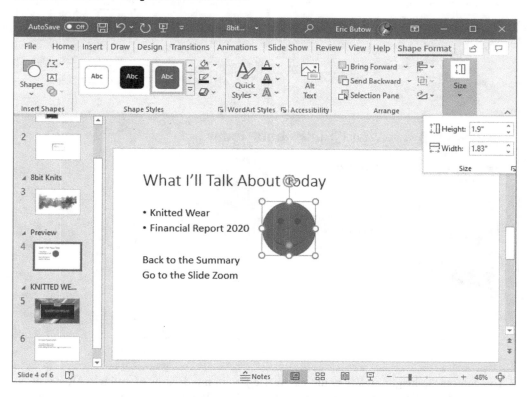

You can set the height and/or width as precisely as in hundredths of an inch. After you type the height and/or width and then press Enter, the size of the shape changes in the slide.

Resize a Text Box

You can resize a text box manually by clicking anywhere in the text box, clicking and holding one sizing handle around the boundary of the text box, and then dragging the text box until it's the size you want.

If you want to set the exact height and/or width of the shape, type the measurement in inches in the Height and/or Width boxes, as shown in Figure 3.28. (If your PowerPoint window width is small, click the Size icon in the Shape Format ribbon and then type the height and/or width.)

FIGURE 3.28   Height and Width boxes in the Size section

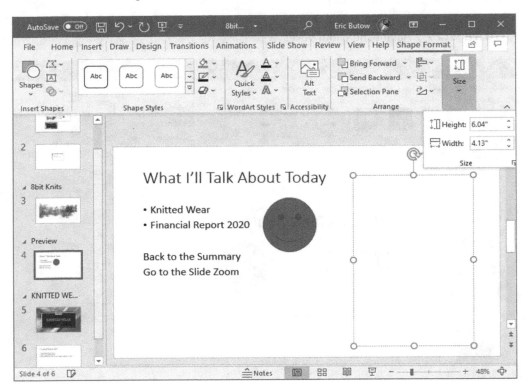

You can set the height and/or width as precisely as in hundredths of an inch. After you type the height and/or width and then press Enter, PowerPoint changes the size of the text box in the slide.

Formatting Shapes and Text Boxes

When you want to format shapes and text boxes, you can do so by clicking the shape or text box and then clicking the Shape Format menu option.

Shapes

Within the Shape Format menu ribbon, shown in Figure 3.29, you can make a variety of changes to the shape, including the following:

FIGURE 3.29   Shape Format ribbon

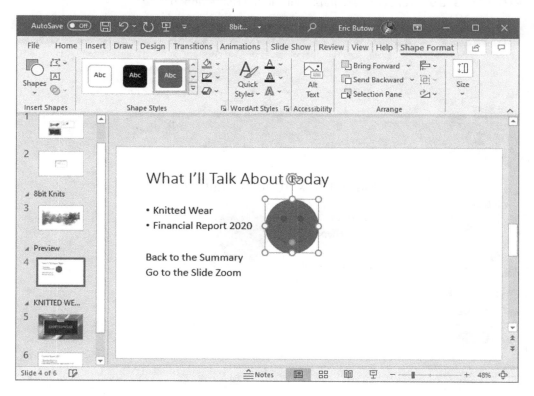

- Changing the shape or editing points in the shape by clicking Edit Shape in the Insert Shapes section
- Changing shape styles, including the shape fill, outline, and effects, in the Shape Styles section
- Changing the size of the shape by typing the height and/or width in the Size section as discussed earlier in this chapter

Text Boxes

If you want to format other features of your text, such as the font and paragraph settings, you can format text in a text box just as you would in the rest of your document.

Start by selecting the text in the text box that you want to edit. Next, click the Home menu option (if necessary). In the Home ribbon, shown in Figure 3.30, you can change the font and paragraph as you see fit within the Font and Paragraph options. (If your PowerPoint window width is small, you need to click the Font or Paragraph icon to open the drop-down menus and view the editing options.)

FIGURE 3.30   Font and Paragraph icons in the Home ribbon

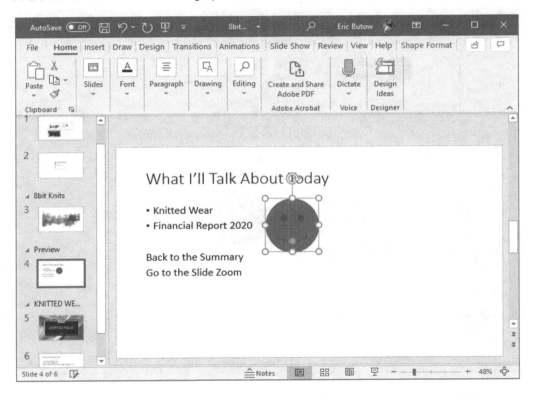

Placing Your Graphics for Easy Reading

Your boss has reviewed your slideshow and she likes it—mostly. She wants to add more shapes on slides so that people can get different representations of each function of the great new product that the company is rolling out. For example, she wants circles with text inside so that each circle points out an important new feature.

There is a limit to the number of graphics that you should add to a document so as not to overwhelm viewers and leave them wondering where they should look . . . or ignore the graphics completely. A reader's eyes follow a pattern as they look across a slide—from the upper-left corner to the lower-right corner, and then to the lower-left corner.

So, if you want to get the attention of your customers (and please your boss), position your graphics in one or more of those locations in your document. When readers visually scan those graphics, they will likely pick up on some of the text that you have in your slide, too.

Applying Built-In Styles to Shapes and Text Boxes

After you add a shape or a text box, you can change the style of the shape. If you have text within a shape or text box, you can change the text within the shape or text box as well as how the text appears.

Apply a Shape Style

You can apply a shape style in the Shape Styles section, as shown in Figure 3.31.

FIGURE 3.31   Shape Styles section

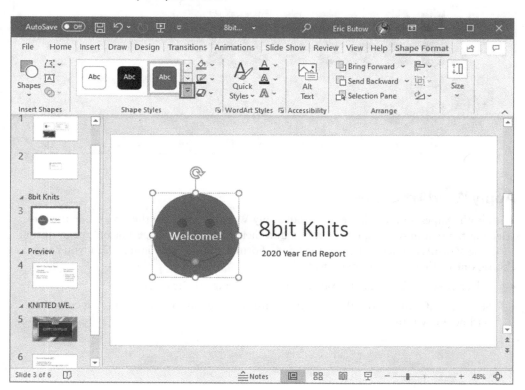

Each style in the style row shows different shape backgrounds, borders, and text colors. If you don't see the style you want, click the More button to the right of the last tile in the style row highlighted in Figure 3.31. It looks like a down arrow with a line above it.

The complete list of built-in style tiles in the drop-down menu appears (see Figure 3.32). Select one of the tiles in the list to apply it to the shape.

FIGURE 3.32 Shape Styles drop-down list

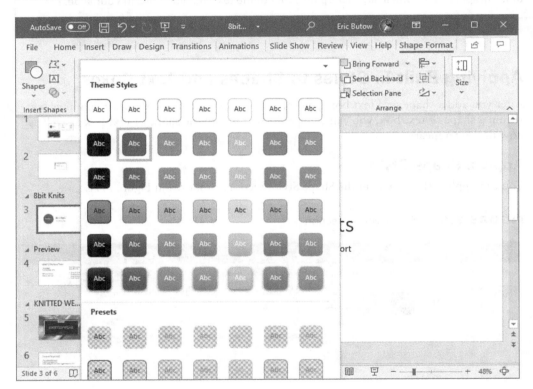

Apply WordArt Styles

With both shapes and text boxes, you can apply WordArt styles to the text inside them by selecting the text in the shape or text box and then clicking the Shape Format menu option.

In the WordArt Styles section in the Shape Format ribbon (see Figure 3.33), you can choose one of three built-in text effects:

- Select Text Fill from the drop-down menu to change the text color.

- Select Text Outline from the drop-down menu to add an outline, including color and outline line width.

- Select Text Effects to view and add other effects to the text. In the drop-down menu, move the mouse pointer over one of the effects to see how each effect appears in your photo. You can choose from Shadow, Reflection, Glow, Bevel, 3-D Rotation, and Transform.

FIGURE 3.33   WordArt Styles section

Change Text Appearance

You can change the text appearance in your shape or text box by clicking the shape or text box and then clicking the Home menu option (if necessary).

In the Paragraph section in the Home ribbon, shown in Figure 3.34, you can change the text appearance in one of three ways:

- Click Text Direction to rotate the text 90 degrees or 270 degrees. You can also click Stacked to display the text with all letters stacked on top of each other in a vertical line.

- Click Align Text to align the text vertically with the Top, Middle, or Bottom of the shape. The default is Middle.

- Click Convert To SmartArt to display your text in one of 20 built-in graphic layout formats, such as an organizational chart.

FIGURE 3.34 Paragraph section

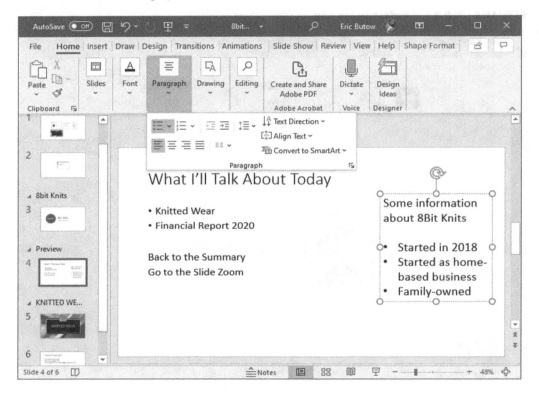

If your PowerPoint window width is small, you need to click the Paragraph icon to open the drop-down menus and view paragraph editing options.

Adding Alt Text to Graphic Elements for Accessibility

Alt text, or alternative text, tells anyone who views your document in PowerPoint what the picture or shape is when the reader moves their mouse pointer over it. If the reader can't see your document, then PowerPoint will use text-to-speech in Windows to read your Alt text to the reader audibly.

Here's how to add Alt text:

1. Click the picture or shape.
2. Click the Shape Format or Picture Format menu option.

3. In the Shape Format or Picture Format ribbon, click the Alt Text icon in the Accessibility section.

4. In the Alt Text pane on the right side of the PowerPoint window (see Figure 3.35), type one or two sentences in the text box to describe the object and its context.

FIGURE 3.35   Alt Text pane

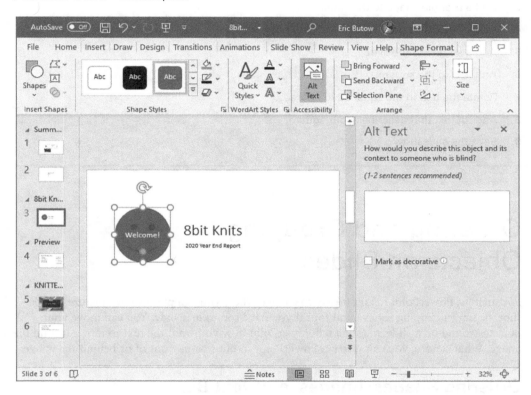

Some images, especially stock images, already have this information in the text box, but you can change it.

5. Click the Mark As Decorative check box if your image, shape, or SmartArt graphic adds visual interest but isn't informative, such as a line.

6. When you're done, close the pane by clicking the Close (X) icon in the upper-right corner of the pane.

EXERCISE 3.4

Inserting and Formatting Graphic Elements

1. Open the slideshow that you created in Exercise 3.1.

2. In the left pane, click the slide where you want to add a shape.

3. Add a triangle shape to the slide.

4. Add text to the square.

5. Add a square to the slide.

6. Add text to the square.

7. Rotate the text in the square 270 degrees.

8. Add Alt text that describes your square.

9. Save the slideshow.

Ordering and Grouping Objects on Slides

Fortunately, PowerPoint makes it easy to change where you can put a shape, picture, screen-shot, or screen clipping (or even all four if you have room) in a slide. You can move your objects around on a slide and then tell PowerPoint how you want the text to move around the image. What's more, you can instruct PowerPoint to put text in front of or behind the image.

Ordering Shapes, Images, and Text Boxes

When you add a new shape, image, or text box, the object appears in front of the rest of the text on the page, if any. Now you can move the shape, image, or text box in your document by moving the mouse pointer over the image, holding down the mouse button, and then moving the image.

If you want the shape, image, or text box to appear in front of or behind other elements, including text, shapes, and images, you can do so by clicking the Home menu option (if necessary). Within the Drawing section, click Arrange. (If your PowerPoint window isn't very wide, click the Drawing icon and then click Arrange.)

The Drawing drop-down list appears, as shown in Figure 3.36.

FIGURE 3.36   Drawing drop-down list options

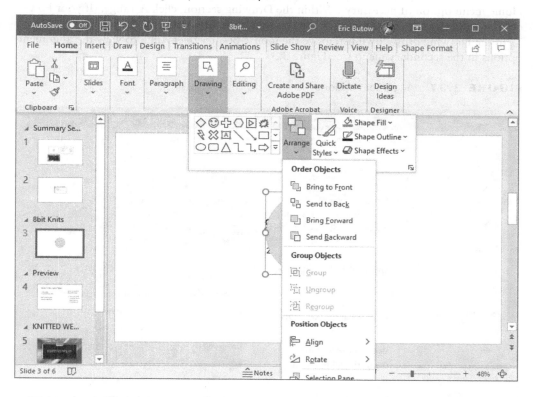

Within the Order Objects section at the top of the drop-down list, you can change the stacking order of a shape, image, or text box in a slide in one of four ways:

Bring To Front: Moves the object to the top layer in the stack. Every other object appears behind the object in front.

Send To Back: Moves the object to the bottom layer in the stack. All other objects appear in front of the object at the bottom layer.

Bring Forward: Moves the object up one layer in the stack

Send Backward: Moves the object down one layer in the stack

Aligning Shapes, Images, and Text Boxes

When you add a new shape, image, or text box, the object appears in front of the rest of the text on the page, if any. Now you can move the shape or image in your document by moving the mouse pointer over the image, holding down the mouse button, and then moving the image.

If you need to align your shape, image, or text box within a slide, start by clicking the Home menu option (if necessary). Within the Drawing section, click Arrange. (If your PowerPoint window isn't very wide, click the Drawing icon and then click Arrange.)

In the Drawing drop-down list, move the mouse pointer over Align to view the alignment options in the secondary menu (see Figure 3.37).

FIGURE 3.37 Alignment options

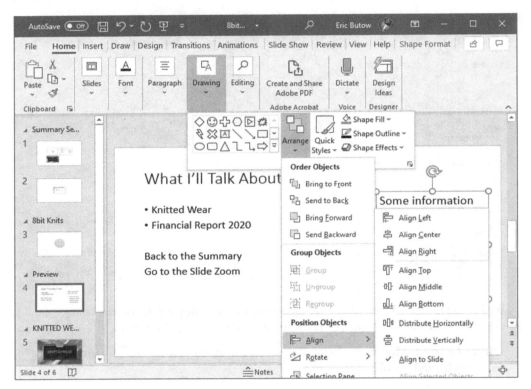

You can change the alignment of a shape, image, or text box in a slide by clicking one of the following six options:

Align Left: Aligns the object at the left side of the slide

Align Center: Aligns the object vertically in the center of the slide

Align Right: Aligns the object at the right side of the slide

Align Top: Aligns the object at the top of the slide

Align Middle: Aligns the object horizontally in the middle of the slide

Align Bottom: Aligns the object at the bottom of the slide

You can click more than one option to align the object both horizontally and vertically within the slide. For example, click Align Center and then click Align Bottom to align the object horizontally in the center bottom of the slide.

Grouping Shapes and Images

You can move several images or shapes by grouping them together. Start by selecting the first object, and then hold down the Ctrl key. Next, select the other images and/or shapes that you want to group.

Now click the Home menu option (if necessary). Within the Drawing section, click Arrange. (If your PowerPoint window isn't very wide, click the Drawing icon and then click Arrange.)

From the Drawing drop-down list, select Group in the Group Objects section (see Figure 3.38).

FIGURE 3.38 Group option in the drop-down menu

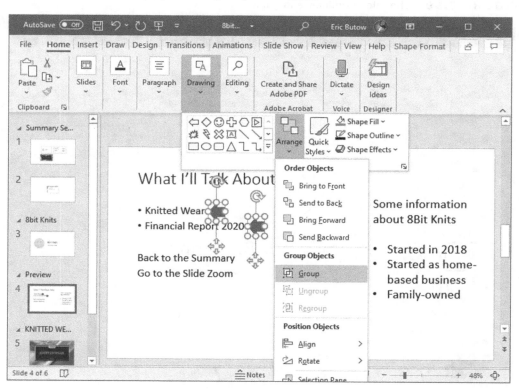

Now you can move all the grouped objects around the slide. You can ungroup them by clicking Arrange in the Home ribbon and then selecting Ungroup from the drop-down menu.

Displaying Alignment Tools

To figure out where you want to align your shape, image, and/or text box within a slide, you can display *guides* and *gridlines* to have PowerPoint give you a good idea of where it places objects. You can also display *rulers* above and to the left of the slide, just as you can in Word.

Display the rulers, guide, and gridlines by following these steps:

1. Click the View menu option.
2. In the Show section in the View ribbon, select the Ruler check box. (If your PowerPoint window isn't very wide, click the Show icon and then select the Ruler check box.)
3. Select the Gridlines check box.
4. Select the Guides check box.

Now you see the rulers, the gridlines with dotted lines throughout the slide, and the guides with dashed lines through the vertical and horizontal center of the slide (see Figure 3.39).

FIGURE 3.39 The ruler, gridlines, and guides

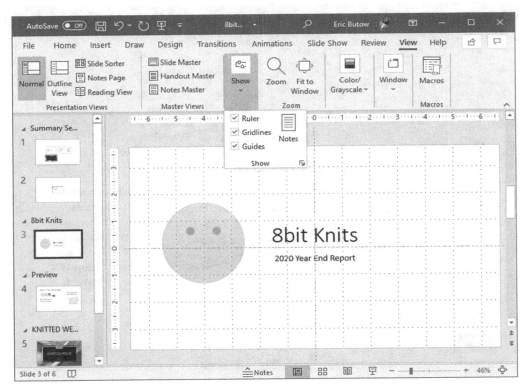

As you move an object around the slide, the object will snap to a point in the slide and highlight the gridline or guide. For example, if you move a shape to the horizontal center of the slide, the horizontal guide appears in red when the object snaps to the guide.

You can hide the rulers, gridlines, and/or guides by repeating steps 2, 3, and/or 4 depending on what you want to hide.

EXERCISE 3.5

Ordering and Grouping Objects on Slides

1. Open the slideshow that you created in Exercise 3.4, if necessary.

2. Align the triangle at the top center of the slide.

3. Align the square at the middle center of the slide.

4. Order the shapes so that the triangle is in front of the square.

5. Select and group both shapes.

6. Display the guides in the slide.

7. Position the group so that the shapes appear in the center of the slide, both vertically and horizontally.

8. Save the slideshow.

Summary

This chapter started with a discussion on how to format shapes, images, and text boxes. You learned how to apply formatting and styles to text within shapes and text boxes, format text in your slide within multiple columns, as well as create bulleted and numbered lists.

I followed up by discussing how to insert hyperlinks, Section Zoom links, and Slide Zoom links. Then you learned how to resize and crop images in a slide, add built-in styles and effects to images, insert screenshots, and add screen clippings to a slide.

Next, you learned how to insert and format shapes and text boxes, draw on a slide, add text to shapes and text boxes, and add Alt text to a graphic object to ensure that people who can't see that object will know what that image, shape, screenshot, or screen clipping is about.

Finally, you learned how to order shapes and images on a slide, including ordering, aligning, and grouping shapes and images. You also learned how to display alignment tools on a slide to help you place the shape and/or image.

Key Terms

Alt text	pictures
digital ink	rulers
Format Painter	screen clippings
gridlines	screenshots
guides	Section Zoom
indent	Slide Zoom
picture effect	spacing
picture style	

Exam Essentials

Understand how to format text.   PowerPoint allows you to apply styles and other text formatting, format text in multiple columns, and create both bulleted and numbered lists.

Know how to insert different types of links.   Understand how to insert hyperlinks, Section Zoom links, and Slide Zoom links, and know the differences between all three link types.

Be able to add and format different types of graphics.   PowerPoint allows you to add a variety of shapes and photos to your slideshow. You need to know how to add shapes, pictures, screenshots of open windows, and clip portions of your screen to your slideshow. You also need to know how to resize and crop images as well as apply built-in styles and effects to an image.

Know how to draw on a slide.   Be able to use digital ink within PowerPoint to draw directly onto a slide to make a point and/or annotate a slide.

Understand how to insert and format shapes and text boxes.   Know how to add a shape, resize and format a shape, apply built-in styles to a shape, and insert text into a shape.

Know how to add and format text boxes.   Understand how to add a text box that is separate from other text on a page, modify a text box, and format text in a text box.

Be able to add Alt text.   Understand why Alt text is important for your readers and know how to add Alt text to a graphic or picture.

Understand how to order and group shapes, images, and text boxes on slides.   Know how to order objects so that they appear above or below other objects, align objects in a slide, group shapes and images, and display alignment tools including rulers, gridlines, and guides.

Review Questions

1. How do you apply a format from one selected block of text to another block?
   A. By clicking the Format Painter icon in the Home ribbon and selecting the other block
   B. By seeing what style the block of text has in the Home ribbon or Styles text
   C. By searching for the special character in the Navigation pane
   D. From the Symbol window

2. How does a link appear in your slide?
   A. Blue text
   B. Bold text
   C. Blue and underlined text
   D. Underlined text

3. How do you apply a specific picture style in the Picture Format ribbon?
   A. Click the Corrections icon.
   B. Click one of the picture styles tiles in the Picture Styles area.
   C. Click Picture Effects.
   D. Click Change Picture.

4. Why should you add a text box?
   A. Because it's easier to read
   B. Because you need to add one before you can start typing text in the slide
   C. You don't need to add one because you can add text directly on a slide
   D. To have text separate from the rest of the text in your slideshow

5. What ordering tool do you use when you want to move an object down a level in the stack?
   A. Send To Back
   B. Align Bottom
   C. Send Backward
   D. Align Middle

6. When you add a link to a Summary Zoom slide, what options do you have to select in the Insert Hyperlink dialog box? (Choose all that apply.)
   A. Existing File Or Web Page
   B. Place In This Document
   C. The first named slide title in the page
   D. The numbered slide that corresponds to the Summary Zoom slide

7. What menu option do you click to change the indentation and spacing of text in a slide?

A. Home

B. Shape Format

C. View

D. Design

8. How do you add text to a shape?

A. Use the Shape Format ribbon.

B. Click the Draw ribbon.

C. Use the Insert ribbon.

D. Right-click the shape.

9. Why should you add Alt text to shapes and images?

A. Because it's required for all images in a PowerPoint slideshow

B. To help people who can't see the shape or image know what the shape or image is about

C. Because PowerPoint won't save your document until you do

D. Because you want to be as informative as possible

10. What are the three alignment tools that you can display in a slide? (Choose all that apply.)

A. Guides

B. Gridlines

C. Slide Master

D. Rulers

Chapter

4

Inserting Tables, Charts, SmartArt, 3D Models, and Media

MICROSOFT EXAM OBJECTIVES COVERED IN THIS CHAPTER:

✓ **Insert tables, charts, SmartArt, 3D models, and media**

- Insert and format tables
    - Create and insert tables
    - Insert and delete table rows and columns
    - Apply built-in table styles
- Insert and modify charts
    - Create and insert charts
    - Modify charts
- Insert and modify SmartArt graphics
    - Insert SmartArt graphics
    - Convert lists to SmartArt graphics
    - Add and modify SmartArt graphic content
- Insert and modify 3D models
    - Insert 3D models
    - Modify 3D models
- Insert and manage media
    - Insert audio and video clips
    - Create and insert screen recordings
    - Configure media playback options

Tables are effective in conveying information in a slide that your audience can digest easily. This chapter begins by showing you how to create tables. You will also learn how to insert and delete rows and columns from a table, as well as apply built-in table styles.

Then I will show you how to create a chart in a slide. You will also see how to modify charts by adding data series, switch between rows and columns, and add and modify various chart elements.

Next you will learn about custom diagrams—which Microsoft calls SmartArt—so that you can add things like organization and process charts easily. You will also learn how to convert lists to SmartArt graphics as well as add and modify SmartArt content.

I will then show you how to insert 3D models, either from your own computer or from stock libraries installed with PowerPoint.

Finally, you'll learn how to insert and manage different types of media in a PowerPoint slideshow, including audio and video; how to create screen recordings; and how to configure media playback options.

Inserting and Formatting Tables

PowerPoint makes it easy for you to create a table within a slide. When you need to change your table, PowerPoint provides plenty of tools to make your table look the way you want, including inserting and deleting rows and columns and the ability to add built-in table styles.

Creating and Inserting Tables

Insert a *table* into a slide by following these steps:

1. In the left pane, click the slide in which you want to create a chart, or create a new slide, as you learned to do in Chapter 2, "Managing Slides."

2. Place your cursor in the content section of the slide (the large section underneath the smaller title section).

3. Click the Insert menu option.

4. Click the Table icon.

5. Move your mouse pointer over the grid in the drop-down menu. Cells in the grid light up as you move the pointer so that you can see the size of the table in terms of *rows* and *columns*.

The table also appears in your slide so that you can see what the table will look like as you move the mouse pointer over the grid in the drop-down menu.

6. When the table is the size you want, click the highlighted cell, as shown in Figure 4.1.

FIGURE 4.1 The selected table cells

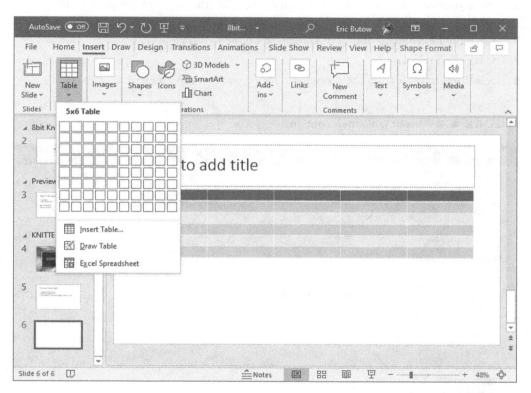

Now the table appears on the page with the number of rows and columns you selected in the grid.

Inserting and Deleting Table Rows and Columns

The Insert Table grid gives you the ability to create a maximum table size of only 10 columns and 8 rows. You can insert as many as 75 rows and 75 columns into a table. You can also insert and delete one or more rows or columns in a table.

Create a Larger Table

If you need more rows or columns than what the Insert Table grid will allow, follow these steps:

1. In the left pane, click the slide in which you want to create a chart, or create a new slide, as you learned to do in Chapter 2.

2. Place your cursor in the content section of the slide (the large section underneath the smaller title section).

3. Click the Insert menu option (if you haven't done so already).

4. Click the Table icon.

5. Select Insert Table from the drop-down menu, as shown in Figure 4.2.

FIGURE 4.2   Insert Table menu option

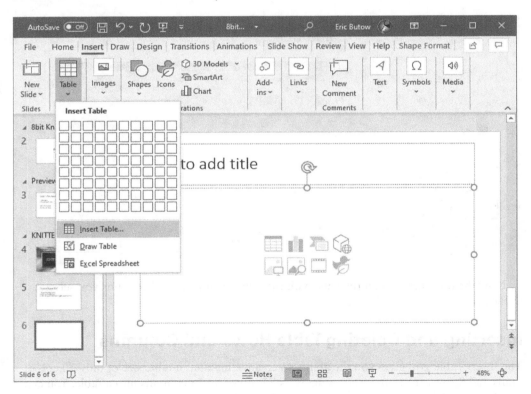

6. In the Insert Table dialog box (see Figure 4.3), specify the number of columns and rows that you want in the Number Of Columns and Number Of Rows boxes, respectively. The default is five columns and two rows.

FIGURE 4.3   Insert Table dialog box

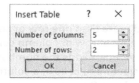

Insert Rows and/or Columns

If you need to insert rows and/or columns after you have created a table, follow these steps:

1. Click a cell within the table. The cursor blinks in your cell within the row or column.

2. Click the Layout menu option.

3. In the Rows & Columns section in the Layout ribbon, shown in Figure 4.4, click one of the four insertion options.

FIGURE 4.4   Insertion options in the Rows & Columns section

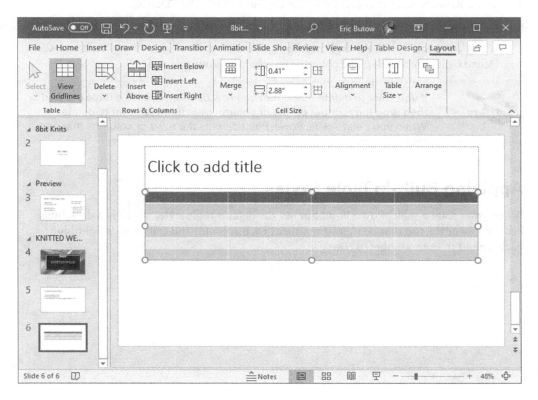

The four insertion options are (from left to right):

Insert Above: Insert a new row above the selected cell.

Insert Below: Insert a new row below the selected cell.

Insert Left: Insert a new column to the left of the selected cell.

Insert Right: Insert a new column to the right of the selected cell.

 If you want to add more than one row or column, click a table cell and then drag the number of row or column cells that you want to add. When you add cells, PowerPoint adds the number of rows or columns. For example, if you select three cells in a column and then insert rows below the selected cells, PowerPoint adds three new rows under the selected cells.

Delete Rows and/or Columns

When you need to delete a row or column, PowerPoint also makes this easy to do. Here's how:

1. Click a cell within the table. The cursor blinks in your selected cell within the row or column.

2. Click the Layout menu option.

3. In the Rows & Columns section in the Layout ribbon, click Delete.

4. From the drop-down menu (see Figure 4.5), select Delete Rows or Delete Columns.

   When you click Delete Rows, PowerPoint deletes the row with your selected cell. Click Delete Columns to delete the column that contains your selected cell.

 If you want to delete more than one row or column, click a table cell and then drag the number of row or column cells that you want to delete. When you delete cells, PowerPoint deletes the rows or columns that contain the cells.

Applying Built-In Table Styles

When you create a table, PowerPoint applies the default table style, which is a dark blue header row at the top that contains the title of each column, and cells with a light blue background in even-numbered rows.

FIGURE 4.5   Delete options

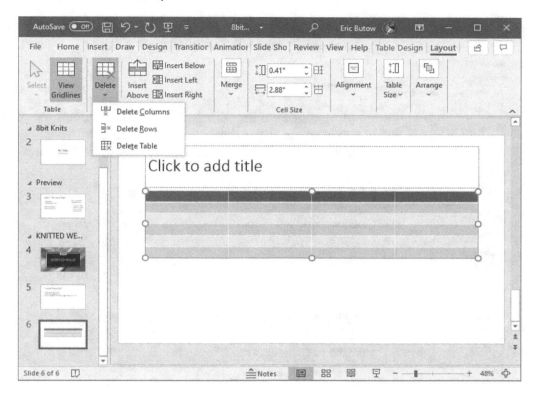

If you prefer to apply a different table style, apply another built-in table style by following these steps:

1.   Click a cell within the table.

2.   Click the Table Design menu option.

3.   In the Table Styles section in the Table Design ribbon, click the More button to the right of the row of table style tiles. (The More button looks like a down arrow with a horizontal line above it.)

4.   From the Table Styles drop-down list, shown in Figure 4.6, select one of the table style tiles.

FIGURE 4.6   Table style tiles

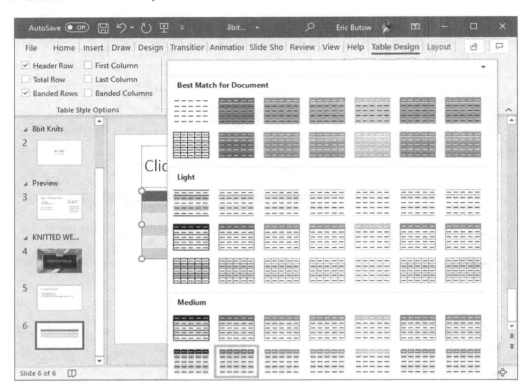

As you move the mouse pointer over each style tile, the table on the slide changes so that you can see what the style will look like before you select it. If you decide that you like the current table style after all, click outside the drop-down menu to close the menu.

EXERCISE 4.1

Inserting and Formatting Tables

1. Open a new slideshow.

2. Create a new Title And Content slide, as you learned to do in Chapter 2.

3. In the content area of the slide, create a new table with six rows and five columns.

4. Click in the third row in the table.

5. Add a new row below the current row.

6. Delete the column.

7. Apply a different style to the table.

8. Save the slideshow.

Inserting and Modifying Charts

PowerPoint is a visual medium, so it should come as no surprise that you can add a chart into a slideshow. After you insert a chart, the built-in chart tools let you modify it, such as adding data series, changing how data is presented, and adding more elements.

Creating and Inserting Charts

So, how do you build a chart? After you open a slideshow and either open a slide or create a new one to place your chart into, follow these steps:

1. In the left pane, click the slide in which you want to create a chart, or create a new slide, as you learned to do in Chapter 2.

2. Place your cursor in the content section of the slide (the large section underneath the smaller title section).

3. Click the Insert menu option.

4. In the Illustrations section in the Insert ribbon, click the Chart icon, as shown in Figure 4.7.

FIGURE 4.7   The Chart icon in the Insert ribbon

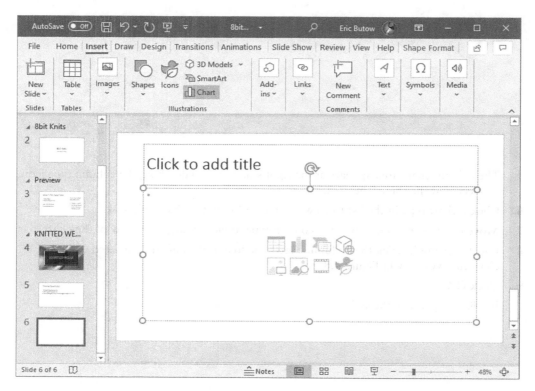

5. In the Insert Chart dialog box that appears (see Figure 4.8), the Column category is selected in the list on the left side of the dialog box.

FIGURE 4.8   The Column category in the Insert Chart dialog box

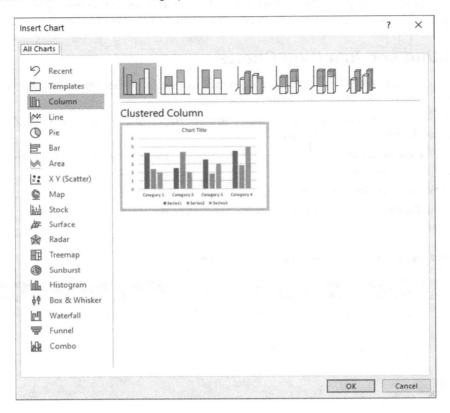

The column chart area appears at the right side of the dialog box; the column type icon is selected at the top of the area.

6. Click a chart type in the list to view a sample of how the chart will look.

7. Move the mouse pointer over the column type to view a larger preview of the chart.

8. For this example, click the Column chart type to add the default Clustered Column chart that you saw in Figure 4.8.

9. Click OK.

The chart appears in the slide, as shown in Figure 4.9.

FIGURE 4.9   The chart in the worksheet

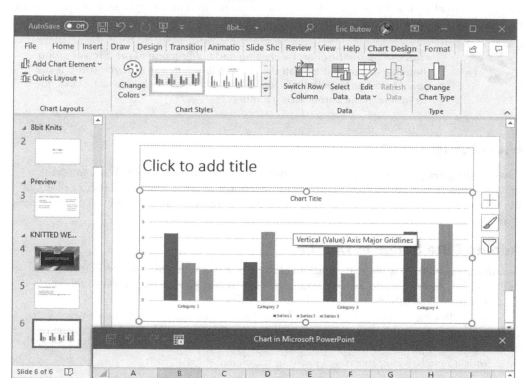

A Chart In Microsoft PowerPoint window appears underneath the chart and on top of the PowerPoint window (see Figure 4.10). That shows you a small spreadsheet with all of the numeric values in the chart selected.

FIGURE 4.10   The selected chart entries in the spreadsheet window

	A	B	C	D	E	F	G	H	I	
		Series 1	Series 2	Series 3						
1										
2	Category 1	4.3	2.4	2						
3	Category 2	2.5	4.4	2						
4	Category 3	3.5	1.8	3						
5	Category 4	4.5	2.8	5						

The window remains on the screen even if you click outside the chart or even on another slide. You can close the window by clicking the Close (X) icon at the right side of the window title bar that you saw in Figure 4.10.

 You can resize the chart by clicking and holding one of the circular sizing handles and then dragging the chart in the direction that you want. If you want to resize both the horizontal and vertical size of the chart, click and drag one of the corner sizing handles.

Modifying Charts

PowerPoint gives you a lot of power to modify your charts as you see fit. You can sort text and/or numbers in a table. You can also take advantage of more tools to change the look of the text and graphics in your chart, align your chart in the worksheet, and even change the chart type.

Adding Data Series to Charts

A *data series* is one or more rows and/or columns in a worksheet that PowerPoint uses to build a chart. After you add a chart, you may want to add more information to the worksheet and have PowerPoint update the chart accordingly.

Start by clicking the chart if necessary. Then type text and/or numbers in a new row or column. PowerPoint adds a new element to the chart that reflects the new data automatically. In the example shown in Figure 4.11, a new series of data in column E of the spreadsheet adds a new bar in each category within the chart.

 In Figure 4.11, the spreadsheet window has been moved above the chart so that you can see both the spreadsheet and the chart.

Switching Between Rows and Columns in Source Data

PowerPoint follows one rule when it creates a chart: the larger number of rows or columns is placed in the horizontal axis. For example, if there are 12 columns and 5 rows, then columns are along the horizontal axis.

But what if you want the rows to appear in the horizontal axis? Here's what to do:

1. Click the chart in the slide.
2. Click the Chart Design menu option.
3. In the Data section in the Chart Design menu ribbon, click Switch Row/Column.

FIGURE 4.11   The updated chart and expanded selection area in the spreadsheet

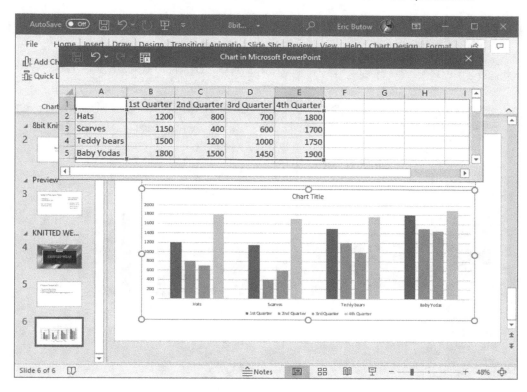

Now the axes have switched, as you can see in Figure 4.12, so that you can determine whether you like it. If you don't, click Switch Row/Column in the Chart Design ribbon again.

As you switch between rows and columns, keep the following in mind:

- If the Switch Row/Column icon is disabled, it means that you don't have the Chart In Microsoft PowerPoint window open. You can open this window by right-clicking in the chart and then clicking Edit Data in the pop-up menu.

- What happens if you have equal numbers of rows and columns in your worksheet or table? PowerPoint uses the same layout as rows and columns in a worksheet: columns for the horizontal axis and rows for the vertical axis.

FIGURE 4.12   Column titles in the horizontal axis

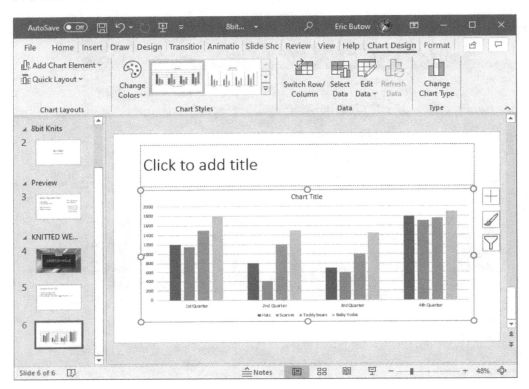

Adding and Modifying Chart Elements

It's easy to add and modify the elements that you see in a chart. You can view a list of elements that you can add to the chart by clicking anywhere in the chart and then clicking the Chart Elements icon at the upper-right corner of the chart.

A list of the elements appears, with check boxes to the left of each element name, as shown in Figure 4.13.

Selected check boxes indicate that the element is currently applied. Cleared check boxes mean that the element is not applied. When you move the mouse pointer over the element in the list, you see how the element will appear in the chart—that is, if the element is not already applied.

The following is a list of the elements that you can add and remove from your chart:

Axes   These are the horizontal and vertical units of measure in the chart. In the sample chart shown in Figure 4.13, the horizontal units represent products sold and the vertical units represent sales in increments of 200. PowerPoint shows the axes by default.

FIGURE 4.13   Chart elements list

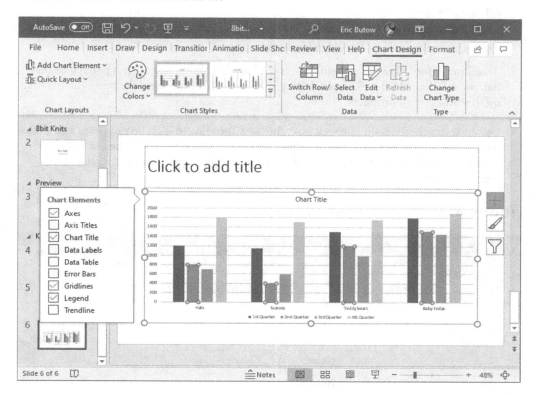

Axis Titles   These are the titles for the vertical and horizontal axes. The default name of each title is Axis Title. You can change the title after you add it by double-clicking within the title, selecting the text, and then typing your own text.

Chart Title   PowerPoint automatically shows the title of your chart, which is Chart Title by default. You can change this title by double-clicking Chart Title, selecting the text, and then typing a new title.

Data Labels   These add the number in each cell above each corresponding point or bar in the chart. If your points or bars are close together, having data labels can be difficult to read because the numbers can overlap.

Data Table   PowerPoint places your selected cells in a table below the chart. If you have a large table, then you may need to enlarge the size of the chart in the worksheet.

Error Bars   If you have a chart with data that has margins of error, such as political polls, you can add *error bars* to your chart to show those margins. Error bars also work when you want to see the standard deviation, which measures how widely a range of values are from the mean.

Gridlines   This displays the gridlines behind the lines or bars in a graph. Gridlines are active by default.

Legend   PowerPoint shows the *legend*, which explains what each line or bar color represents, at the bottom of the chart by default.

Trendline A *trendline* is a straight or curved line that shows the overall pattern of the data in the chart. In the example shown in Figure 4.14, I can view the trendline for first quarter sales of all products.

Once I select the Trendlines check box, the Add Trendline dialog box appears and asks me to click the series that I want to check. After I click Quarter 1 in the list and then click OK, the dashed line appears and the trendline also appears in the legend (see Figure 4.14).

FIGURE 4.14   Trendline for first quarter sales

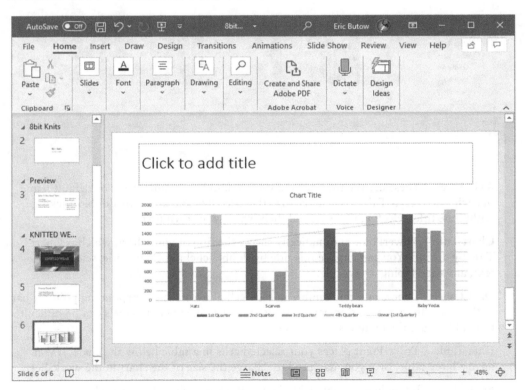

Change Elements More Precisely

An arrow appears to the right of each element name. When you click the arrow, a secondary menu with more precise options, as well as an option for viewing even more options, appears, as shown in Figure 4.13. For example, you can hide the vertical axis label but keep the horizontal axis label.

When you click More Options in the secondary menu, the Format panel appears at the right side of the PowerPoint window so that you can make even more specific changes, such as making the chart title text outlined instead of solid.

EXERCISE 4.2

Inserting and Modifying Charts

1. Open the slideshow that you created in Exercise 4.1 if it's not already open.

2. Create a new Title And Content slide, as you learned to do in Chapter 2.

3. Insert a new slide into the content area of the slide.

4. Add a new chart spreadsheet in the Chart window that includes five rows and four columns.

5. Add text in the first row and in the first column.

6. Add numbers into the remaining cells in the spreadsheet.

7. Create a Clustered Column chart for the entire table.

8. Reverse the axes.

9. Add a new column and populate it with text in the first row and numbers in the other four rows.

10. Add a trendline.

11. Save the slideshow.

Inserting and Formatting SmartArt Graphics

SmartArt graphics are built-in art types for conveying specific kinds of information, such as a flowchart to show a process or a decision tree to show a hierarchy. PowerPoint allows you to create a SmartArt graphic quickly and insert it into a slide. Then you can use built-in tools to format your SmartArt graphic easily.

Inserting SmartArt Graphics

Follow these steps to add a SmartArt graphic:

1. In the left pane, click the slide in which you want to add a SmartArt graphic, or create a new slide, as you learned to do in Chapter 2.

2. Place your cursor in the content section of the slide (the large section underneath the smaller title section).

3. Click the Insert menu option.

4. In the Illustrations section in the Insert ribbon, click SmartArt (see Figure 4.15).

5. In the Choose A SmartArt Graphic dialog box, shown in Figure 4.16, select a category from the list on the left side of the dialog box.

   The default is All, which shows all the SmartArt graphics from which you can choose. The list of SmartArt graphic type icons in the center of the dialog box depends on the category you chose. For this example, I chose Hierarchy.

6. Click the graphic type that you want to insert. A description of the graphic type appears at the right side of the dialog box.

7. Click OK.

The graphic appears in the content section of the slide. You'll learn how to set up a graphic to look the way you want, as well as change the text wrapping style, later in this chapter.

Converting Lists to SmartArt Graphics

When you have a bulleted or numbered list that you want to show graphically, PowerPoint makes it easy to convert a list to a SmartArt graphic. Here's how:

1. In the left pane, click the slide in which you want to add a SmartArt graphic, or create a new slide, as you learned to do in Chapter 2.

2. Place your cursor in the content section of the slide (the large section underneath the smaller title section).

FIGURE 4.15 SmartArt option in the Insert ribbon

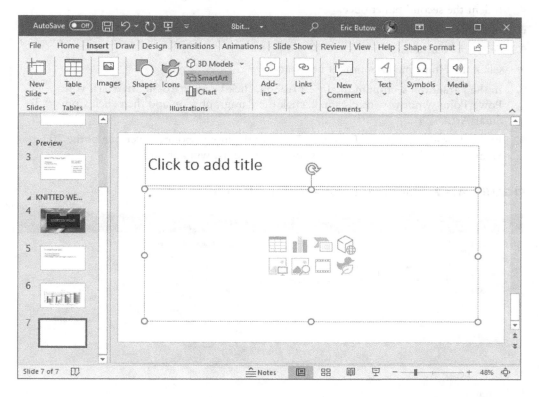

FIGURE 4.16 SmartArt categories

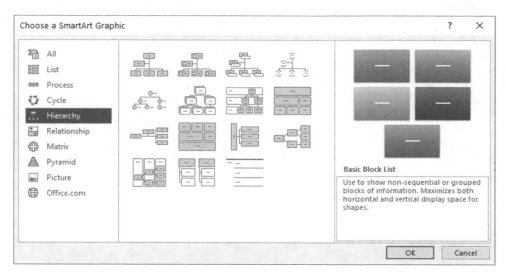

3. If necessary, type a bulleted list with three entries.

4. Indent the second bullet once.

5. Indent the third bullet twice.

6. Select the entire list.

7. Click the Home menu option, if necessary.

8. In the Paragraph section in the Insert ribbon, click Convert To SmartArt. (If your PowerPoint window width is small, click the Paragraph icon and then click Convert To SmartArt.)

9. In the drop-down list (see Figure 4.17), move the mouse pointer over one of the 20 SmartArt graphic tiles to see how your converted list will appear.

FIGURE 4.17   The Convert To SmartArt drop-down list

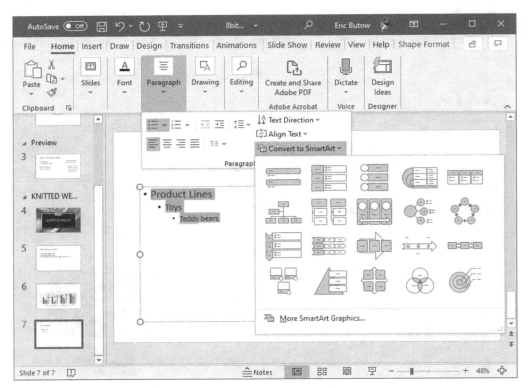

10. When you find a graphic you like, click it.

The graphic appears in the content section of the slide.

> If you don't find a SmartArt graphic that you like, click More SmartArt Graphics at the bottom of the drop-down list. The Choose A SmartArt Graphic dialog box appears so that you can find a graphic to your liking, as you learned about earlier in this chapter.

Adding and Modifying SmartArt Graphic Content

After you add SmartArt, the Type Your Text Here box appears to the left of the image. You can type the text that will appear in the image by clicking [Text] in each bullet line and replacing that template text with your own (see Figure 4.18).

FIGURE 4.18   The Type Your Text Here box

The SmartArt Design ribbon appears by default so that you can make any changes you want. The type of SmartArt you added determines the options that appear in the ribbon.

For example, I created an organization chart, shown in Figure 4.19, and in the ribbon, I can change the following:

- The layout of the chart in the Create Graphic section
- The layout type in the Layouts section
- The chart box colors and styles in the SmartArt Styles section

Remove all graphic style changes that you made and return the graphic to its original style by clicking the Reset Graphic icon.

When you finish making any changes to your SmartArt graphic, click the page outside the graphic to deselect it.

FIGURE 4.19   Designing an organization chart using SmartArt

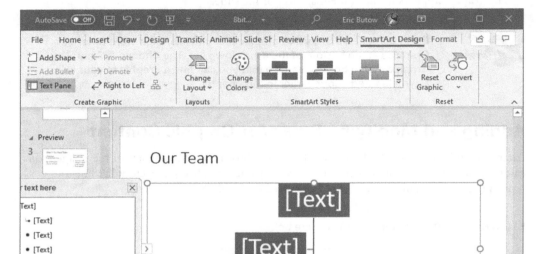

 As you modify your SmartArt graphic, remember these points:

- Once you stop editing your SmartArt graphic and deselect it, you won't be able to remove any previous changes that you made to the graphic.

- Convert the SmartArt graphic to a text or shape by clicking Convert in the Reset section in the SmartArt Design ribbon.

- You can change the size of a SmartArt graphic or screen clipping image by clicking the image, moving the mouse pointer over one of the circular handles on the perimeter of the image, holding down the mouse button, and dragging the image. When the image is the size you want, release the mouse button.

Inserting and Formatting SmartArt Graphics

1. Open the slideshow that you created in Exercise 4.1 if it's not already open.

2. Create a new Title And Content slide, as you learned to do in Chapter 2.

3. Click within the content area of the slide.

4. Create a bulleted list with four entries.

5. Convert the list to a Vertical Block List SmartArt graphic.

6. Change two of the text entries in the SmartArt graphic.

7. Change the SmartArt Style into a Subtle Effect in the SmartArt Design ribbon.

8. Save the slideshow.

Inserting and Modifying 3D Models

PowerPoint, Word, and Excel all have access to the Microsoft library of Office graphics. One category of graphics are 3D models.

3D models are graphics that appear three-dimensional on the screen. You can also rotate them by 360 degrees within PowerPoint so that you can have the 3D model oriented the way you want. For example, you may want to have a dinosaur walking away from you rather than toward you.

Inserting 3D Models

You can insert a 3D model into a slide and then change the orientation. Follow these steps:

1. In the left pane, click the slide in which you want to add a SmartArt graphic, or create a new slide, as you learned to do in Chapter 2.

2. Place your cursor in the content section of the slide (the large section underneath the smaller title section).

3. Click the Insert menu option.

4. In the Insert ribbon, click 3D Models in the Illustrations section.

5. You can search for 3D models on your computer or stock 3D models that were installed with PowerPoint. For this example, I'll click Stock 3D Models.

6. In the Online 3D Models dialog box (see Figure 4.20), scroll up and down the list of categories and then click the category tile that you want. I selected the Winter category.

7. Click the 3D model you want and then click Insert.

The model appears in the slide, as shown in Figure 4.21.

FIGURE 4.20 3D model category list

FIGURE 4.21 A 3D hat model

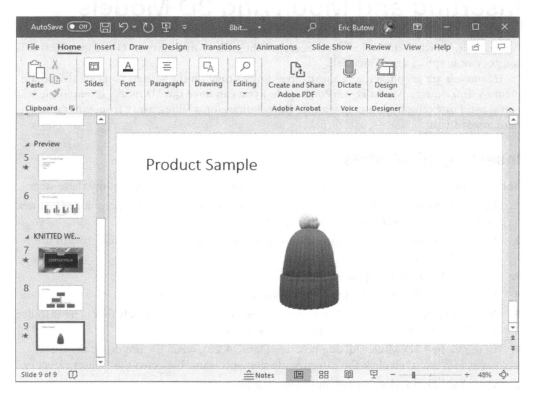

If you have any text on the slide, the model appears in front of the text. You'll learn how to modify the location and position of the 3D model, as well as change the text wrapping style, later in this chapter.

Modifying 3D Models

You can change the size of a 3D model by clicking the model, clicking one of the circular sizing handles on the perimeter of the selection box, holding down the mouse button, and then dragging. When the model is the size you want, release the mouse button.

Rotate the 3D model 360 degrees in any direction by clicking and holding down the Rotate icon in the middle of the model graphic (see Figure 4.22) and then dragging the mouse pointer to see how the model moves. When the model looks the way you want on the slide, release the mouse button.

FIGURE 4.22   The Rotate icon in the 3D model

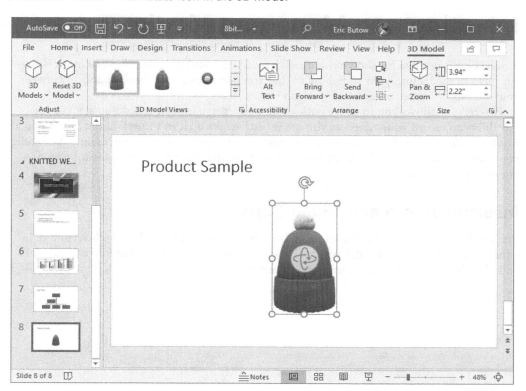

EXERCISE 4.4

Inserting and Modifying 3D Models

1. Open the slideshow that you created in Exercise 4.1 if it's not already open.

2. Create a new Title And Content slide, as you learned to do in Chapter 2.

3. Click within the content area of the slide.

4. Add a new 3D model of your choice.

5. Rotate the model until it looks the way that you want.

6. Save the slideshow.

Inserting and Managing Media

PowerPoint is not just for showing static slides with text and graphics. You can insert different types of media into your slideshow so that you don't have to go back and forth between your slideshow and an external application to run media.

PowerPoint allows you to insert both audio and video clips into a slideshow, gives you the ability to record your screen as you use it (such as for a video tutorial about how to do a task), and then insert the screen recording into a slide. Once you insert media into your slide, you can configure the playback options so that the media plays the way you want it to during your presentation.

Inserting Audio and Video Clips

You can insert just an audio clip into a slide or insert a video clip with or without audio. In either case, PowerPoint includes playback controls within the slide so that you can pause and play the clip during the presentation as needed.

Supported Audio and Video Formats

PowerPoint will insert several different formats of audio and video files, and Microsoft recommends specific audio and video format files for the best results.

For audio files, Microsoft recommends that you insert M4A format files encoded with AAC audio. PowerPoint will also insert audio with the following formats and their associated file extensions:

AIFF audio file: `.aiff`

AU audio file: `.au`

MIDI: `.mid` or `.midi`

MPEG3 audio file: `.mp3`

MPEG4 audio file: `.mp4`

Windows audio file: `.wav`

Windows Media audio file: `.wma`

For video clips, Microsoft recommends that you insert MP4 format files encoded with H.264 video and AAC audio. You can also insert a file with the following formats and their associated file extensions:

Windows Video file: `.asf` or `.avi`

MP4 video file: `.m4v` or `.mov`

MPEG movie file: `.mpg` or `.mpeg`

Windows Media Video file: `.wmv`

If you need more information, search for PowerPoint supported file formats on the Microsoft Support website at `support.microsoft.com`.

Adding an Audio Clip

Insert an audio clip by following these steps:

1. In the left pane, click the slide in which you want to insert the audio clip, or create a new slide, as you learned to do in Chapter 2.

2. Place your cursor in the content section of the slide (the large section underneath the smaller title section).

3. Click the Insert menu option.

4. In the Insert ribbon, click Audio in the Media section. (If your PowerPoint window width is smaller, click Media in the ribbon and then select Audio from the drop-down menu.)

5. Click Audio On My PC (see Figure 4.23).

FIGURE 4.23   Audio On My PC menu option

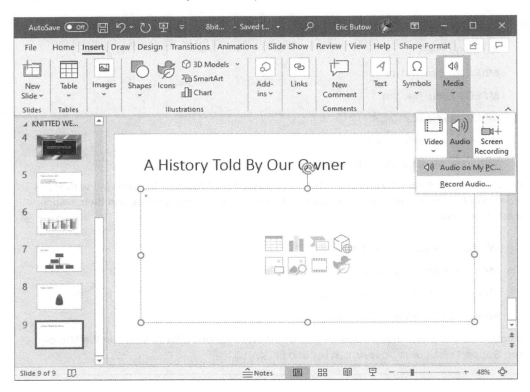

6. In the Insert Audio dialog box, navigate to the folder that contains the audio file you want to insert.

7. Click the name in the list and then click Insert (see Figure 4.24).

FIGURE 4.24   The Insert button in the dialog box

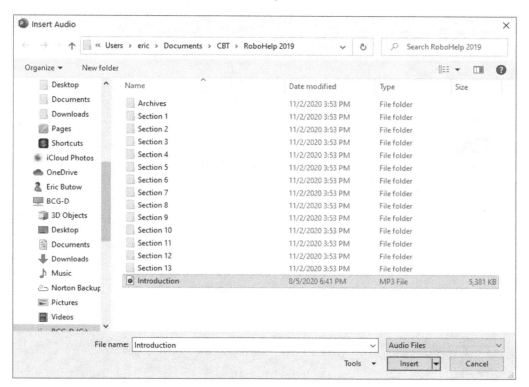

The audio icon appears in the center of the slide with a playback bar underneath it so that you can start playing the audio by clicking the play button (the triangle pointing to the right) at the left side of the playback bar, as shown in Figure 4.25.

After you insert the audio clip, you see sizing handles around the edge of the audio icon. You can resize the size of the icon by clicking and holding on one of the circular sizing handles and then dragging the icon until it's the size you want. This does not affect the playback ability of the audio clip.

The sizing handles also tell you that the audio clip is selected. After you click the audio clip to select it, delete the clip by pressing Delete on your keyboard.

FIGURE 4.25   The audio file in the slide

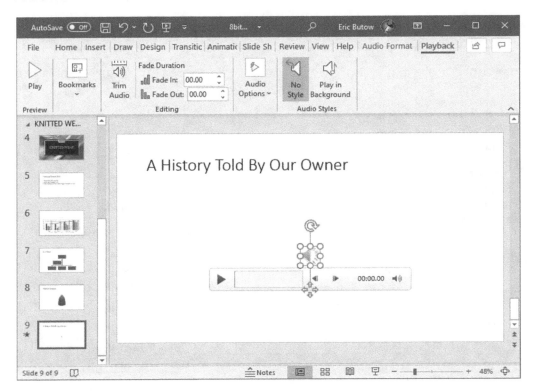

Adding a Video Clip

PowerPoint allows you to embed a video that you have on your computer hard drive or a network into a slide. Insert a video clip by following these steps:

1. In the left pane, click the slide in which you want to insert the video clip, or create a new slide, as you learned to do in Chapter 2.

2. Place your cursor in the content section of the slide (the large section underneath the smaller title section).

3. Click the Insert menu option.

4. In the Insert ribbon, click Video in the Media section. (If your PowerPoint window width is smaller, click Media in the ribbon and then click Video in the drop-down menu.)

FIGURE 4.26   Video On My PC menu option

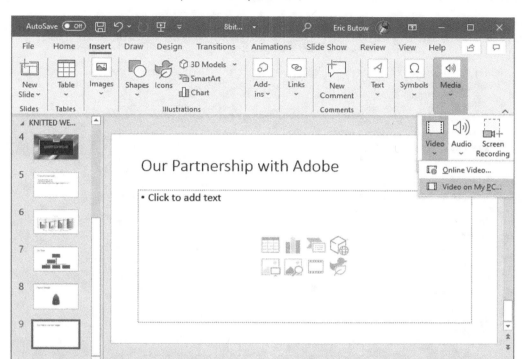

5. Click Video On My PC, as shown in Figure 4.26.
6. In the Insert Video dialog box, navigate to the folder that contains the audio file that you want to insert.
7. Click the name in the list and then click Insert (see Figure 4.27).

FIGURE 4.27   The Insert button in the dialog box

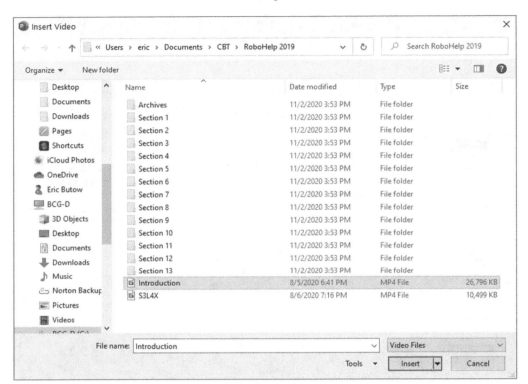

The first frame in the video file appears in the center of the slide with a playback bar underneath it so that you can start playing the video by clicking the play button (the triangle pointing to the right) at the left side of the playback bar (see Figure 4.28).

> After you insert the video clip, you see sizing handles around the edge of the video icon. You can resize the size of the icon by clicking and holding on one of the circular sizing handles and then dragging the icon until it's the size that you want. This does not affect the playback ability of the video clip.
>
> The sizing handles also tell you that the video clip is selected. After you click the video clip to select it, delete the clip by pressing Delete on your keyboard.

FIGURE 4.28 The video file in the slide

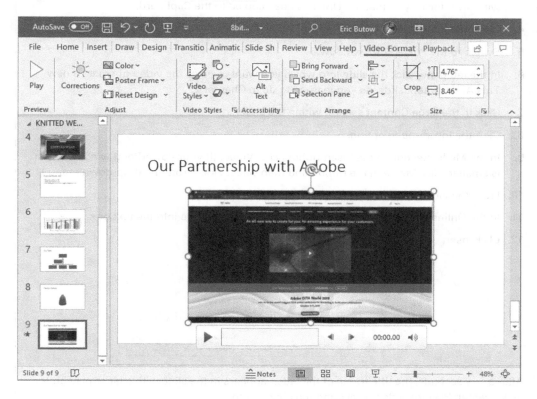

Insert Online Video from YouTube

Your boss has seen a video on YouTube that she thinks would be a great addition to the presentation scheduled to be made to the board of directors the next day. She's given you a mission: embed that YouTube video onto a new slide and save the slideshow on the company intranet so that she can review it.

After you work with your boss and/or anyone else in your company (like the legal department) to make sure that you have permission to use that video in your presentation, PowerPoint makes the rest of the job easy. Just follow these steps:

1. Open the video on YouTube.

2. Click the Share icon underneath the viewer.

3. Click Copy in the Share dialog box. A small box in the lower-left corner of the browser window informs you that the URL has been copied to the Clipboard.

4. Close the dialog box.

5. Switch to the PowerPoint window.

6. In the left pane, click the slide into which you want to place the video or create a new Title And Content slide, as you learned to do in Chapter 2.

7. Click in the large Content section within the slide.

8. Click the Insert menu option.

9. In the Media Section in the Insert ribbon, click Video. (If your PowerPoint window width is smaller, click Media in the ribbon and then select Video from the drop-down menu.)

10. From the Video drop-down list, select Online Video.

11. In the Online Video dialog box, paste the URL from YouTube into the text box.

12. Click Insert.

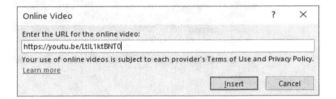

After a few seconds, the title frame of the video appears in the slide with a large play button in the center. Play the video by clicking the Play button.

When you play the video, all of the YouTube video controls appear within the window so that you can change the volume, move the playback slider, and use all the other standard features found in the viewer on the YouTube website.

Creating and Inserting Screen Recordings

If you want to record a screen that shows you doing something in Windows and then insert that recording into a slide, you don't need to use a separate program to do that. PowerPoint has all of the built-in tools so that you can record video and/or audio, as well as audio only.

The directions in this section presume that you have a microphone so that you can record audio.

Recording Audio Clips

Here's how to use audio clips to create and insert an audio recording:

1. In the left pane, click the slide in which you want to insert the audio clip, or create a new slide, as you learned to do in Chapter 2.

2. Place your cursor in the content section of the slide (the large section underneath the smaller title section).

3. Click the Insert menu option.

4. In the Insert ribbon, click Audio in the Media section. (If your PowerPoint window width is smaller, click Media in the ribbon and then select Audio from the drop-down menu.)

5. Click Record Audio (see Figure 4.29).

FIGURE 4.29   Record Audio menu option

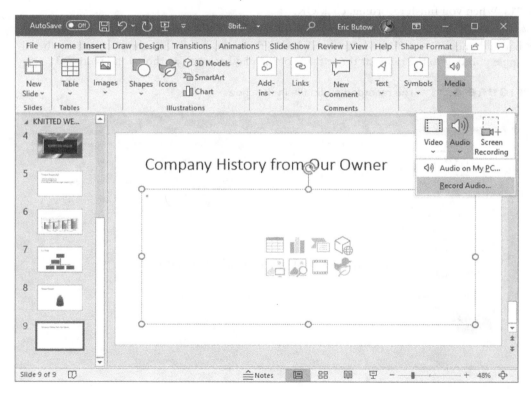

6. In the Record Sound dialog box, shown in Figure 4.30, delete the default Recorded Sound name in the Name box and replace it with a name of your choosing.

7. Click the Record button, which has a red circle icon.

FIGURE 4.30 Record Sound dialog box

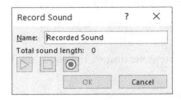

8. Talk into your microphone. As you speak, the Total Sound Length counter starts counting the number of seconds in your recording.

9. When you're done, click the Stop button. (It has a red square icon.)

10. Play back the recording by clicking the Play button, which has a green triangle icon, or resume recording by clicking the Record button.

11. When you finish recording, click OK.

A gray audio icon appears in the center of the slide. Click the icon to show the playback bar underneath it so that you can start playing the audio by clicking the play button (the triangle pointing to the right) at the left side of the playback bar, as shown in Figure 4.31.

FIGURE 4.31 The recorded audio file in the slide

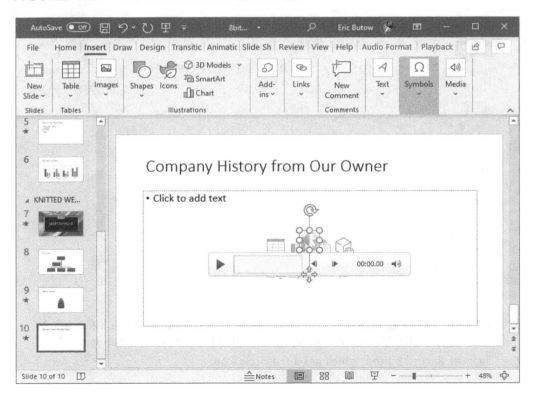

You can move the clip by clicking and holding the audio icon and then dragging the icon to a different location on the slide. If you use more than one audio file on a slide but you want to have your selected audio file appear on multiple slides, it's a good rule of thumb to put that selected audio file in the same location on the slide because PowerPoint doesn't label each individual audio clip.

Recording Video Clips

Record a video clip from within PowerPoint by following these steps:

1. In the left pane, click the slide in which you want to insert the audio clip, or create a new slide, as you learned to do in Chapter 2.

2. Place your cursor in the content section of the slide (the large section underneath the smaller title section).

3. Click the Insert menu option.

4. In the Insert ribbon, click Screen Recording in the Media section, as shown in Figure 4.32. (If your PowerPoint window width is smaller, click Media in the ribbon and then select Audio from the drop-down menu.)

FIGURE 4.32   Screen Recording icon

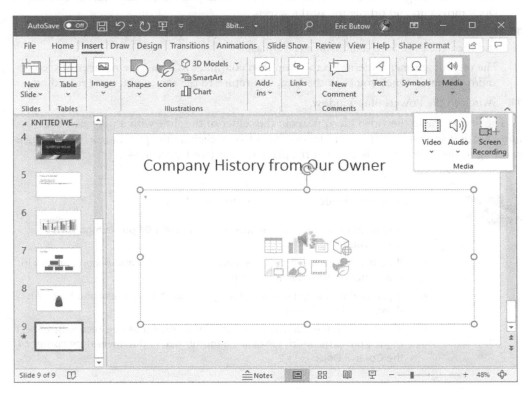

5. In the *Control Dock* box, shown in Figure 4.33, select an area to record by clicking Select Area.

FIGURE 4.33 Control Dock box

PowerPoint adds a slightly opaque white overlay to the entire screen.

6. Click and hold a section in the screen and then drag to select the area to record, which is bounded by a red dashed line.

7. Click Audio to turn off audio recording as you record your video.

8. Click Record Pointer to hide the mouse pointer as you record your video.

9. Click Record.

A large orange box appears in the center of the screen and counts down from three seconds to zero to give you a little time to prepare. Once you start recording, the Control Dock moves up and off the top of the screen.

10. When you're done recording, move the mouse pointer over the top edge of the screen and then click the Stop icon, which is a square.

The recording timer underneath the Stop icon continues to count the number of seconds and/or minutes. Once you click the icon, you return to the screen you were recording.

11. Switch to the PowerPoint window.

The first frame in the video file appears in the center of the slide with a playback bar underneath it so that you can start playing the video by clicking the play button (the triangle pointing to the right) at the left side of the playback bar (see Figure 4.34).

As you create a video recording, note the following:

- You need to record a screen area that is at least 64 pixels high by 64 pixels wide.

- If your video recording contains audio, then a gray audio icon appears in the center of the video in the slide.

- If you prefer to stop recording using your keyboard, press and hold Windows logo key+Shift+Q.

- You can keep the Control Dock from disappearing as you record by clicking the pin icon, which looks like a thumbtack, in the lower-right corner of the Control Dock.

FIGURE 4.34   The video recording and playback bar in the slide

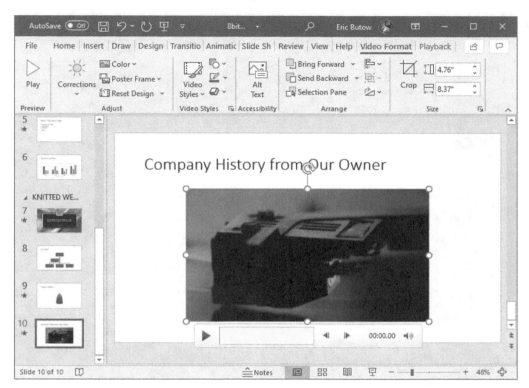

Configuring Media Playback Options

You may not be happy with the audio and/or video you just recorded. For example, you may want to trim off a section at the end of audio that has no sound. PowerPoint gives you rudimentary tools for editing audio and video clips.

Editing Audio Clips

When you click the audio icon in the slide, PowerPoint displays the Playback and Audio Format menu options and displays the Playback ribbon by default (see Figure 4.35).

Within the ribbon, you can click one or more options in the following sections. If your PowerPoint window width is smaller, you may need to click the section name in the ribbon and then select one of the options from the drop-down menu.

FIGURE 4.35 Playback ribbon

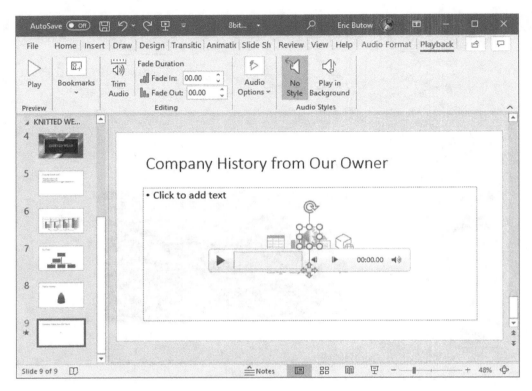

Preview   Click the Play icon to play the audio clip.

Bookmarks   Add a bookmark within the timeline in the playback bar. The timeline is the long bar to the right of the Play button. When you click each bookmark in the timeline, you jump to that point in the audio file.

Trim   Trim the audio by deleting certain parts of the audio file in the Trim Audio dialog box, which is beyond the purview of the MO-300 exam.

Editing   Type the number of seconds to add a fade-in effect at the beginning of the audio clip and/or a fade-out effect at the end of the clip in the Fade In and Fade Out boxes, respectively. You can specify the time as precisely as hundredths of a second.

Audio Options   In this section, you can change the volume, determine how Power-Point should start playing the audio clip, how the audio clip plays, and if the audio icon should be hidden when you play your slideshow.

Audio Styles   Click No Style to reset the playback options to their default settings. You can have the audio play in the background across all slides by clicking Play In Background.

Changing Video Playback Settings

When you insert a video, PowerPoint displays the Video Format and Playback menu options and displays the Video Format ribbon by default. Click the Playback menu option to view the Playback ribbon, as shown in Figure 4.36.

FIGURE 4.36   The Playback ribbon for videos

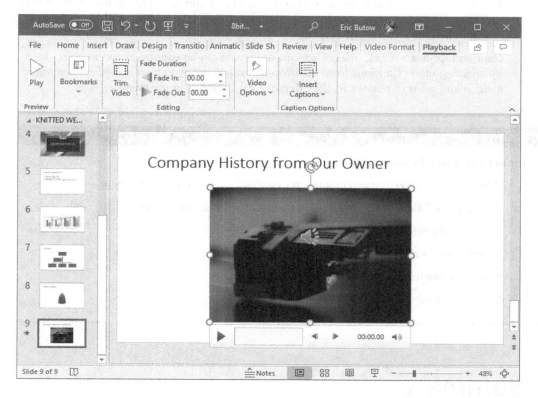

Within the ribbon, you can click one or more options in the following sections. If your PowerPoint window width is smaller, you may need to click the section name in the ribbon and then select one of the options from the drop-down menu.

Preview   Click the Play icon in the Preview section to play the video clip.

Bookmarks   Add a bookmark within the timeline in the playback bar. The timeline is the long bar to the right of the Play button. When you click each bookmark in the timeline, you jump to that point in the video.

Trim   Trim the audio by deleting certain parts of the audio file in the Trim Video dialog box, which is outside the scope of this book and the MO-300 exam.

Editing   Type the number of seconds to add a fade-in effect at the beginning of the video and/or a fade-out effect at the end of the video in the Fade In and Fade Out boxes, respectively. You can specify the time as precisely as hundredths of a second.

Video Options   In this section, you can change the volume, determine how PowerPoint should start playing the audio clip, how the audio clip plays, and if the video should be hidden when the video is not playing.

Caption Options   Click Insert Captions to include closed captioned text in your video by selecting Insert Captions from the drop-down menu. If you have closed captioning in a video and want to remove it, click Remove All Captions in the menu.

EXERCISE 4.5

Inserting and Managing Media

1. Open the slideshow that you created in Exercise 4.1 if it's not already open.
2. Create a new Title And Content slide, as you learned to do in Chapter 2.
3. Add an audio file to the slide.
4. Record a video clip on the slide.
5. Play the video from within the Playback ribbon.
6. Save the slideshow.

Summary

This chapter started by showing you how to create a table and place it in a slide, insert and delete rows and columns within a table, and format your table by applying a built-in table style.

After you created a table, you learned how to create, insert, and modify charts, including adding data series, switching between rows and columns in the chart, and applying a variety of other chart elements.

Next, I discussed how to insert built-in SmartArt graphics to convey your message graphically. You also learned how to convert lists to SmartArt graphics as well as how to add and modify content in a SmartArt graphic.

Then you learned how to insert built-in 3D models into a slide and rotate the orientation of the 3D model.

Finally, you learned how to insert and manage audio and video clips, insert screen recordings, and configure playback options for audio and/or video in a slide.

Key Terms

3D models	legend
chart	rows
columns	SmartArt
Control Dock	Tables
data series	trendline
error bars	

Exam Essentials

Know how to create a table.   Understand how to use the Table option in the Insert menu to insert a table into a slide.

Understand how to modify a table.   Know how to add and delete rows and columns in a table as well as how to change the style of a table by applying a built-in table style.

Know how to add a data series to a chart.   Understand how to add additional cells in a worksheet or a table into a chart after you have already created the chart.

Understand how to switch between row and column data in a chart.   Know how PowerPoint places data series in the horizontal and vertical axes as well as how to switch those axes in a chart.

Know how to add and modify chart elements.   Understand how to add chart elements to your chart—including axes, axis titles, the chart title, data labels in the chart, a data table in the chart, error bars, gridlines, a legend, and a trendline—and be able to modify those elements.

Be able to apply chart layouts. Know how to apply a different chart layout using the Quick Layout menu in the Chart Design ribbon.

Understand how to select and change chart styles. Know how to apply a chart style from the Chart Design ribbon as well as how to change the color scheme for the style.

Understand how to add different types of media. PowerPoint allows you to add a variety of graphics to a slide, including 3D models, SmartArt graphics, audio, and video. You need to know how to add those graphics, audio, and video; modify 3D models and SmartArt graphics; and change audio and video playback options.

Review Questions

1. How do you create a table with built-in styles?
   A. Click the Table icon in the Insert ribbon.
   B. Open the Styles panel.
   C. Click the Insert ribbon, click Table, and then move the mouse pointer over Quick Tables in the drop-down menu.
   D. Click the Columns icon in the Layout menu.

2. If you create a chart that has equal numbers of columns and rows, what does PowerPoint use as the horizontal axis?
   A. A dialog box appears and asks you if you want to use rows or columns.
   B. Columns
   C. Rows
   D. An error message appears in a dialog box.

3. How do you clear style and text changes that you made to a SmartArt graphic?
   A. Use the SmartArt Design menu ribbon.
   B. Delete the SmartArt graphic.
   C. Click the Undo icon in the title bar.
   D. Use the Format menu ribbon.

4. How do you rotate a selected 3D model?
   A. Click one of the icons in the 3D Model Views section in the 3D Model menu ribbon.
   B. Click and drag the handles on the selection box around the model.
   C. Click and drag the icon in the middle of the model.
   D. Click the Position icon in the 3D Model menu ribbon.

5. What keys do you press to stop recording a video? (Choose all that apply.)
   A. Windows logo key+Q
   B. Ctrl+Shift+Q
   C. Windows logo key+Ctrl+Q
   D. Windows logo key+Shift+Q

6. What menu options appear when you click inside a table?
   A. Table Design and Layout
   B. Shape Format
   C. Format and Table Design
   D. Chart Design

7. Why do you add a trendline in a chart?

    A. To show the levels of a bar in a chart better

    B. Because PowerPoint requires it before you can save the chart

    C. To see the overall trend of data over time

    D. To show the margins of error in a chart

8. How do you add a pyramid chart to your document using the Insert menu ribbon?

    A. Click Shapes.

    B. Click SmartArt.

    C. Click Chart.

    D. Click Pictures.

9. When you want to resize a 3D model, what do you select in the 3D Model ribbon? (Choose all that apply.)

    A. Align

    B. Height box

    C. Pan & Zoom

    D. Width box

10. Why do you add bookmarks in an audio or video clip?

    A. To tell you where to trim the clip later

    B. You need to add a bookmark so you can add fade-in and fade-out effects.

    C. Because PowerPoint will not save your slideshow if you don't add at least one bookmark

    D. So you can jump to a particular point in an audio or video clip

Chapter

5

Applying Transitions and Animations

MICROSOFT EXAM OBJECTIVES COVERED IN THIS CHAPTER:

✓ **Apply transitions and animations**

- ▪ Apply and configure slide transitions
  - ▪ Apply basic and 3D slide transitions
  - ▪ Configure transition effects
- ▪ Animate slide content
  - ▪ Animate text and graphic elements
  - ▪ Animate 3D models
  - ▪ Configure animation effects
  - ▪ Configure animation paths
  - ▪ Reorder animations on a slide
- ▪ Set timing for transitions
  - ▪ Set transition effect duration
  - ▪ Configure transition start and finish options

Once you have your slides in order, you may decide that you want to add some pizzazz to your slideshow. PowerPoint allows you to apply built-in options for animating transitions between slides as well as animate models in a slide.

The chapter begins with a discussion about applying various types of slide transitions and how to configure transition effects built into PowerPoint.

Next, I talk about how to animate content in your slide, including text, graphics, and 3D models. You will also learn how to configure animation effects and paths, as well as how to reorder your animations on a slide.

Finally, you'll learn how to change the duration for transition effects between slides and how to configure the transition start and finish options.

Applying and Configuring Slide Transitions

PowerPoint has many built-in slide transitions so that you can transition from one slide to another in a way that will (maybe) impress your audience. Once you add a transition, you can change the transition effects to one of the many built-in effect styles that come with PowerPoint.

The instructions in this section presume that you are working in Normal view within PowerPoint. You can learn more about views in Chapter 1, "Creating Presentations."

Applying Basic and 3D Slide Transitions

When you want to add a transition between slides, follow these steps:

1. In the left pane, click the slide to which you want to add the transition.

2. Click the Transitions menu option.

3. In the Transitions To This Slide section in the Transitions ribbon, click the More button to the right of the row of transition slides. (The More button looks like a down arrow with a line above it.)

4. In the drop-down list, as shown in Figure 5.1, click the transition effect icon from one of three sections: Subtle, Exciting, and Dynamic Content.

FIGURE 5.1 The drop-down list of transition effects

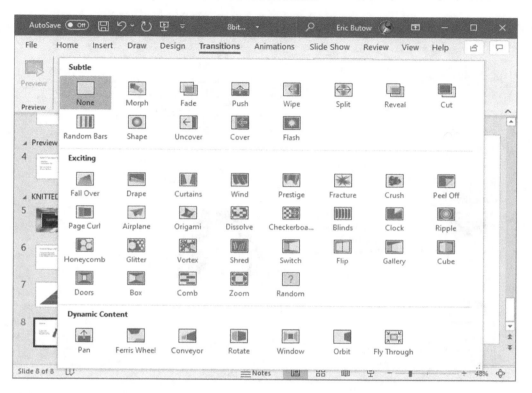

 If you need more information about what an effect does, hover the mouse pointer over the transition effect icon. After a second or two, a tooltip describes what the effect does.

For this example, I used the Rotate effect in the Dynamic Content section, which is an example of a 3D slide transition—that is, the effect makes it appear that the slide is three-dimensional as it rotates from the current slide to the next one.

When you first apply the effect, you see the effect in the slide. However, this effect may go too quickly. You can preview the effect at any time by clicking the Preview icon in the Transitions ribbon (see Figure 5.2).

If you decide that you no longer want to have any effect applied to the slide, click the More button in the Transitions ribbon and then click None in the Subtle section (which is as subtle as it gets).

FIGURE 5.2   Preview icon

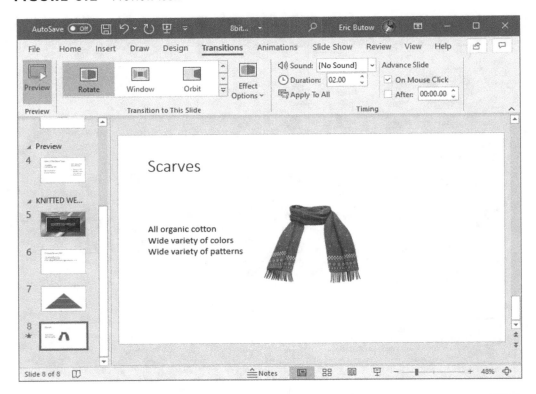

The effect that you select applies only to the current slide. If you want the effect to apply to all slides, click Apply To All in the Timing section in the Transitions ribbon.

Configuring Transition Effects

After you add a transition effect, many (but not all) effects allow you to configure the effect to behave in different ways. Configure a transition effect by following these steps:

1. In the left pane, click the slide that contains the transition you created in the previous section.

2. Click the Transitions menu option.

3. In the Transitions To This Slide section in the Transitions ribbon, click the More button to the right of the row of transition slides. (The More button looks like a down arrow with a line above it.)

4. Click one of the transition options in the drop-down menu. For this example, I choose the Airplane transition (see Figure 5.28).

FIGURE 5.3   Airplane transition in the drop-down list

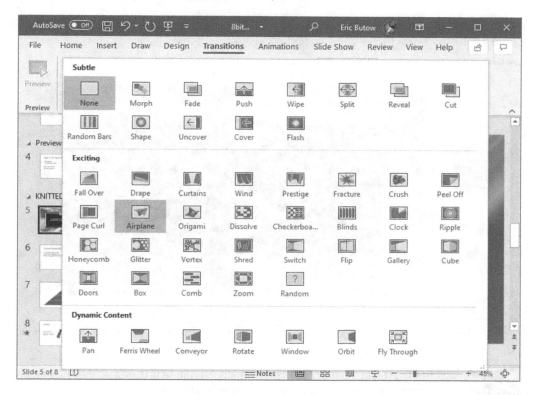

PowerPoint previews the transition so that you can see how the Airplane effect works.

5. In the Transitions To This Slide section in the Transitions ribbon, click Effect Options.

What you see in the Effect Options drop-down list depends on the transition that you select. For the Airplane effect, the default direction of the airplane is Right.

6. Click Left to have the previous slide fold into a paper airplane and fly off the left side of the slide (see Figure 5.4).

PowerPoint animates the slide so that you can see how the transition will appear in your presentation. The duration of the transition may affect how quickly the new effect plays in the slide, and you may need to change the transition timing accordingly.

FIGURE 5.4 The Left icon in the drop-down list

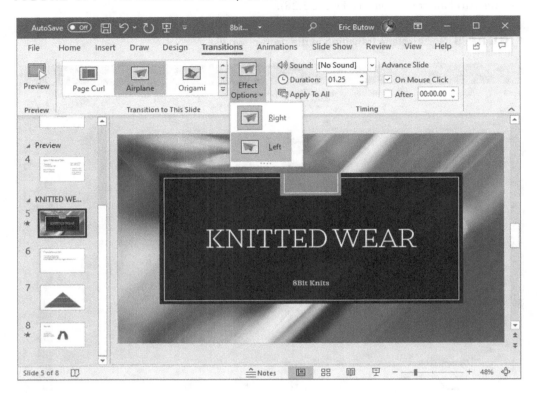

 If the Effect Options icon in the Transitions ribbon is disabled, this means there are no options that you can set for that effect.

 **Real World Scenario**

Add Sounds, Not Just Effects

Your boss likes the effect that you chose for all of your slides. However, she wants to have a sound play during the transition from the first slide to the second. This, she says, will help get the audience to perk up a bit during the early morning presentation.

PowerPoint has you covered with more than a few built-in sounds that you can add to a transition quickly. Here's how to do that:

1. In the left pane, click the slide that contains the transition.

2. Click the Transitions menu option.

3. In the Timing section in the Transitions ribbon, click the down arrow to the right of the No Sound box.

4. In the drop-down menu, click one of the sound effects in the list.

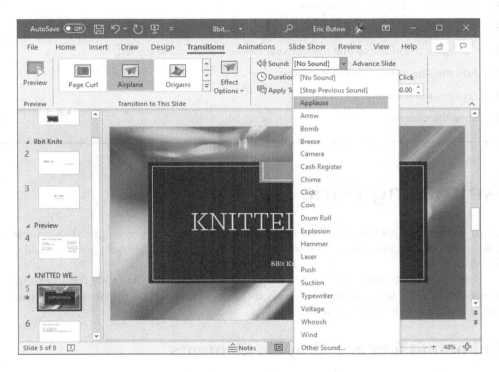

You can listen to the sound with the transition by clicking Preview in the Transitions ribbon.

If you want to add your own sound, such as the company jingle stored on the company intranet, click Other Sound at the bottom of the drop-down menu. You can navigate to the file and insert it within the Add Audio dialog box.

EXERCISE 5.1

Applying and Configuring Slide Transitions

1. Open a new slideshow.

2. Add one slide in addition to the current one. If you need to know how to add slides, refer to Chapter 2, "Managing Slides."

3. Add text to both slides.

4. Click the first slide in the left pane.

5. Add the Conveyor transition effect.

6. Configure the effect so that the Conveyor effect moves from the left.

7. Add the Applause sound to the slide.

8. Preview the transition effect.

9. Save the slideshow.

Animating Slide Content

When you want to get your audience to pay attention to the material on one slide, animating content can be effective. PowerPoint gives you the option to animate text, graphics, and even 3D models.

After you animate your content, you may find that you need to fine-tune the animation to make it look the way you want. PowerPoint contains many effect options to make your animation(s) look the way you want.

Animating Text and Graphic Elements

You can animate text in one of two ways: have one line appear at a time or have one letter appear at a time. You can also animate individual shapes and SmartArt graphics, modify the animation in the Animation pane, reverse the animation order, and remove an animation.

Making Text Appear One Line at a Time

When you want to animate each line of text to appear on the slide one at a time instead of all at once, follow these steps:

1. In the left pane, click the slide with the text that you want to animate.

2. Click in the section of the slide that contains the text.

3. Click the Animations menu option.

4. In the Animation section in the Animations ribbon, click the More button to the right of the row of transition slides. (The More button looks like a down arrow with a line above it.)

If your PowerPoint window width is small, click the Animation Styles icon in the Animations ribbon.

5. In the drop-down list, shown in Figure 5.5, click an animation style icon. For this example, I'll click Float In.

FIGURE 5.5 Animation styles in the drop-down list

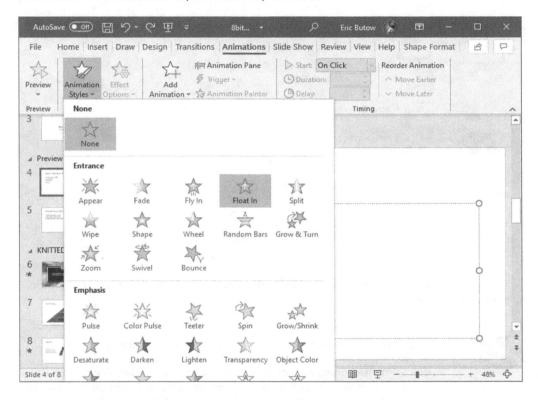

6. In the Animations ribbon, click Effect Options.

By default, PowerPoint shows the Float In effect appearing one line at a time, but the following steps show you how to return to this default option if the effect option is different.

7. At the bottom of the menu, click As One Object to make the text float in at one time.

8. Click Effect Options in the Animations ribbon.

9. Reapply the Float In effect to have the text appear one line at a time by clicking By Paragraph (see Figure 5.6).

FIGURE 5.6 By Paragraph at the bottom of the drop-down list

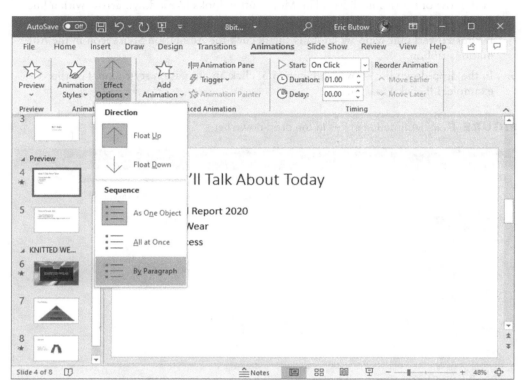

PowerPoint animates the text on the slide so that each line of text floats in one at a time, starting with the top line.

As you create animations, take note of the following features:

- Numbered orange boxes, or *markers*, appear at the left side of each slide that show you how many animations are in the slide and the order of the animations. That is, the number 1 marker means that the first animation runs before the second animation denoted by the number 2 marker.

- Markers on a slide don't appear in your presentation.

- In the left pane, you see a little star icon to the left of the thumbnail-sized slide in the list. Click this icon to play all of the animations in the slide.

- You can also preview all of the animations in the slide by clicking the Preview icon in the Animations ribbon.

Making Text Appear One Letter at a Time

When you make text appear on a slide one letter at a time, this gives your audience the illusion that you're typing text directly into the slide. Follow these steps to add this effect:

1. In the left pane, click the slide with the text that you want to animate.
2. Click in the section of the slide that contains the text.
3. Click the Animations menu option.
4. In the Advanced Animation section in the Animations ribbon, click Animation Pane.

   The Animation Pane appears on the right side of the PowerPoint menu (see Figure 5.7).

FIGURE 5.7   Animation Pane

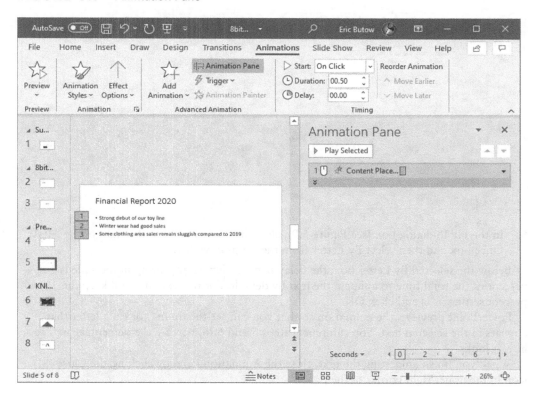

5. Click the down arrow to the right of the text that you want to animate in the list, and then select Effect Options from the drop-down menu, as shown in Figure 5.8.

FIGURE 5.8 Effect Options in the drop-down menu

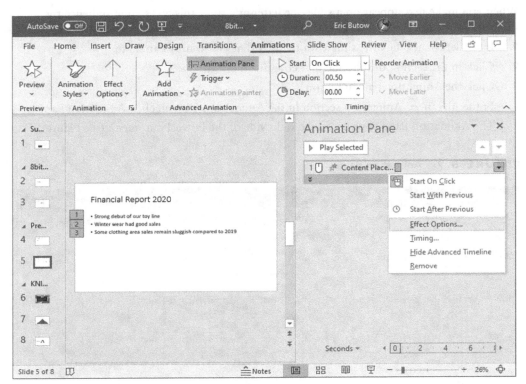

6. In the Fly In dialog box (see Figure 5.9), click the down arrow to the right of the All At Once box and then select By Letter from the drop-down list.

Below the selected By Letter box, the delay between letters appearing in the slide is 10 percent of the total time to animate the text by default. For this example, I'll keep the 10 percent setting as is and click OK.

PowerPoint previews the animation so that you can see the timing for each letter that appears in the selected text. You can repeat steps 5 and 6 to increase the percentage and see how it looks.

When you finish animating the text, close the Animation Pane by clicking the Close (X) icon in the upper-right corner of the pane.

If the animation went by too quickly for you, preview it again by clicking Preview in the Animations ribbon.

FIGURE 5.9 By Letter option in the Animate Text drop-down menu

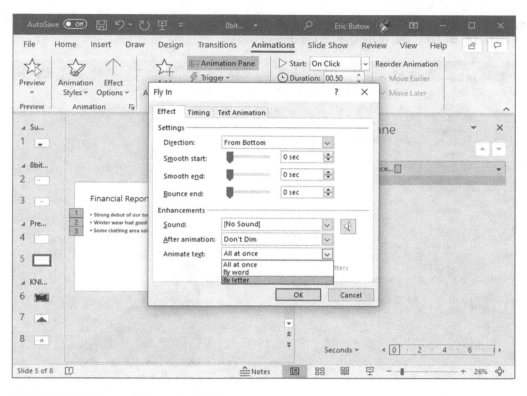

Animating SmartArt Graphics

PowerPoint allows you to animate SmartArt graphics and individual shapes within them. For example, you may want to animate one part of a graphic at a time to help make a point.

Here's how to add a SmartArt graphic and animate it:

1. In the left pane, click the slide in which you want to add the SmartArt graphic.

2. Click in the slide and then click the Insert menu option.

3. In the Illustrations section in the Insert ribbon, click SmartArt.

4. Select the graphic that you want to add in the Choose A SmartArt graphic and then click OK. This example uses a pyramid.

5. Click the Animations menu option.

6. In the Animation section in the Animations ribbon, click the More button to the right of the row of transition slides. (The More button looks like a down arrow with a line above it.)

    If your PowerPoint window width is small, click the Animation Styles icon in the Animations ribbon.

7.   In the drop-down list, as shown in Figure 5.10, click an animation style icon. For this
     example, I'll click Wipe.

FIGURE 5.10   The Wipe style in the drop-down list

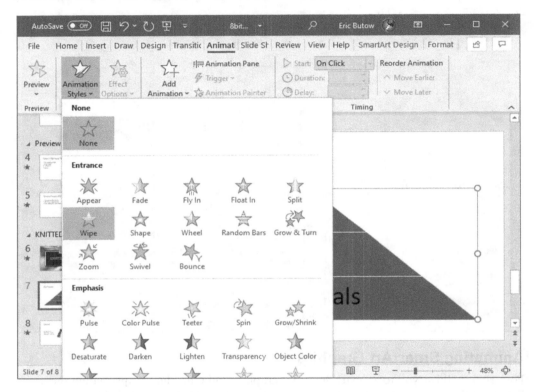

You can select an animation style from one of three sections: Entrance, Emphasis, and
Exit. The Wipe style icon in this example is in the Entrance section.

After you click Wipe, PowerPoint animates the SmartArt graphic so that you can see how
it will look in your presentation. You will learn how to configure animation effects for a
SmartArt graphic later in this chapter.

 You can get more information about adding a SmartArt graphic in
Chapter 4, "Inserting Tables, Charts, SmartArt, 3D Models, and Media."

Animating Shapes in a SmartArt Graphic

Now that you have animated an entire SmartArt graphic, you can animate individual shapes
within it. In the pyramid example I created, I will animate the various levels of the pyramid
by clicking Effect Options in the Animation section in the Animation ribbon.

From the drop-down list shown in Figure 5.11, select One By One.

FIGURE 5.11   One By One option in the Sequence section

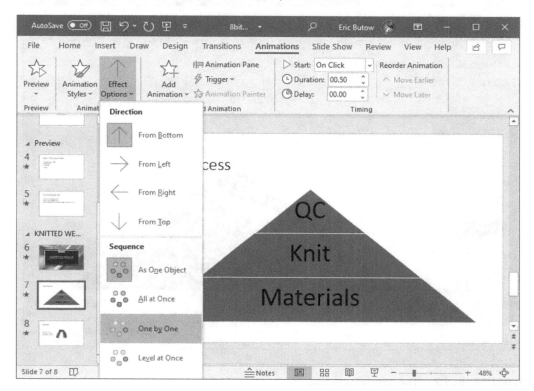

PowerPoint previews the animation on the slide so that you can see each shape gradually appear in the SmartArt graphic. You will learn how to control the timing of the animation later in this chapter.

Reverse the Order of an Animation

In this example, the animation appears with each level in the pyramid appearing from top to bottom, and each level appears from the bottom to the top. You can reverse the order of the animation so that the pyramid appears from the bottom to the top by following these steps:

1. Click the SmartArt graphic in the slide, if necessary.
2. Click the Animations menu option, if necessary.
3. In the Animation section in the Animations ribbon, click the Show Additional Effects Options icon in the lower-right corner of the section (see Figure 5.12).
4. In the Wipe dialog box, shown in Figure 5.13, click the SmartArt Animation tab.
5. Click the Reverse Order check box.
6. Click OK.

FIGURE 5.12   The Show Additional Effects Options icon

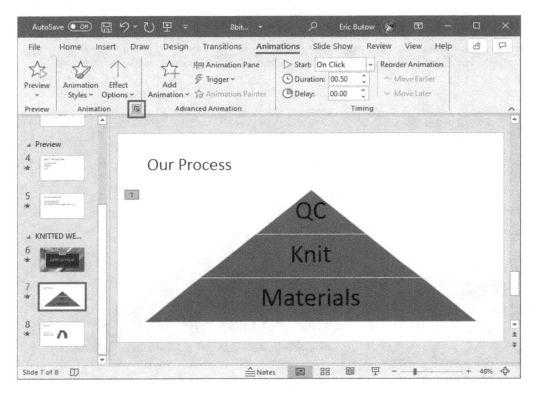

FIGURE 5.13   The Wipe dialog box

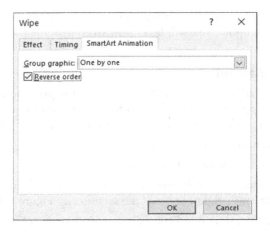

After you click OK, PowerPoint previews the animation that shows each level appearing from the bottom to the top.

 You cannot reverse the animation for an individual shape within a SmartArt graphic. You can only reverse all of the shapes.

Removing an Animation

When you want to remove an animation from one or all levels of an animation, such as all the levels of a pyramid in this example, follow these steps:

1. Click the SmartArt graphic in the slide, if necessary.
2. Click the Animations menu option, if necessary.
3. Click the Animations menu option.
4. In the Advanced Animation section in the Animations ribbon, click Animation Pane.
5. Click the down arrow to the right of the text for level 1 (see Figure 5.14).
6. Select Remove from the drop-down menu, as shown in Figure 5.15.

FIGURE 5.14   Level 1 in the Animation Pane

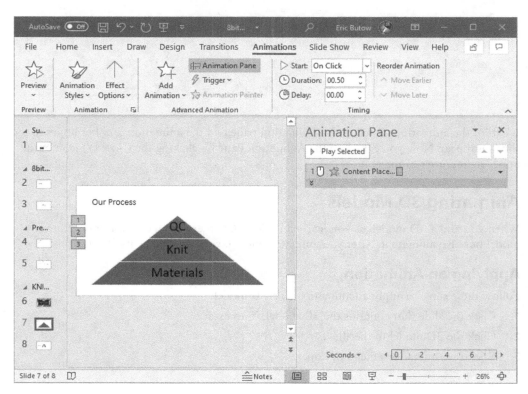

FIGURE 5.15   Remove option in the drop-down menu

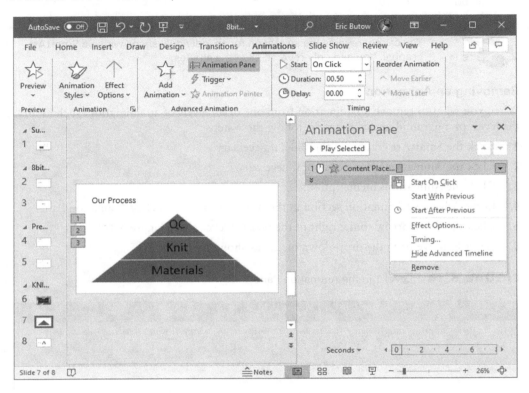

All of the animations listed in the Animation pane and the animation number boxes in the slide disappear. Now you can close the Animation Pane by clicking the Close (X) icon in the upper-right corner of the pane.

Animating 3D Models

When you add a 3D model, as you learned to do in Chapter 4, you can not only rotate a model but also animate it. After you animate a model, you can change its effects.

Applying an Animation

Follow these steps to apply an animation to a 3D model:

1. Click the slide that contains the 3D model, if necessary.
2. Click the 3D model in the slide.
3. Click the Animations menu option.

4. In the Animation section in the Animations ribbon, click the More button to the right of the row of transition slides. (The More button looks like a down arrow with a line above it.)

   If your PowerPoint window width is small, click the Animation Styles icon in the Animations ribbon.

5. In the drop-down list, as shown in Figure 5.16, click an animation style icon in the 3D section at the top of the list. For this example, I'll click Turntable.

FIGURE 5.16   The Turntable style in the drop-down list

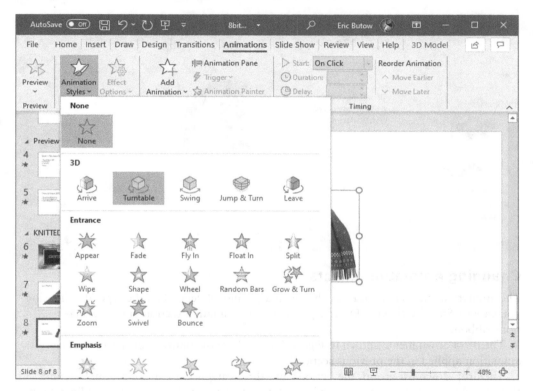

After you click Turntable, PowerPoint previews the SmartArt graphic animation. In this example, you see the 3D model of a scarf (see Figure 5.17) rotate around the x-axis in the slide.

FIGURE 5.17   The rotating scarf with the Turntable effect applied

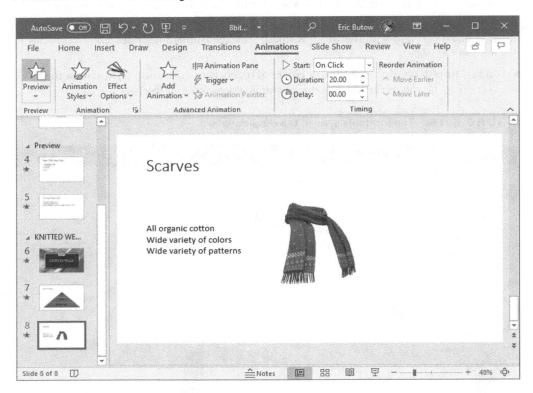

Changing Animation Effects

The animation effects that you can change in a 3D model depend on the type of animation you choose. Start by clicking Effect Options in the Animation section in the Animations ribbon.

The drop-down menu, shown in Figure 5.18, reflects the options for the Turntable animation applied in the previous section.

The drop-down list groups the options into three categories: Direction, Amount, and Rotation Axis. (You may see options in the Intensity category for some effects.) By default, the options for the Turntable effects are to rotate to the right, do a full spin of the 3D model, and spin on the View Center rotation axis.

Change one of these options by clicking the option(s) in the drop-down menu. For example, click Down to rotate the 3D model on the z-axis. After you click the option, PowerPoint previews the new animation effect in the slide.

FIGURE 5.18 Animation effect options for the Turntable style

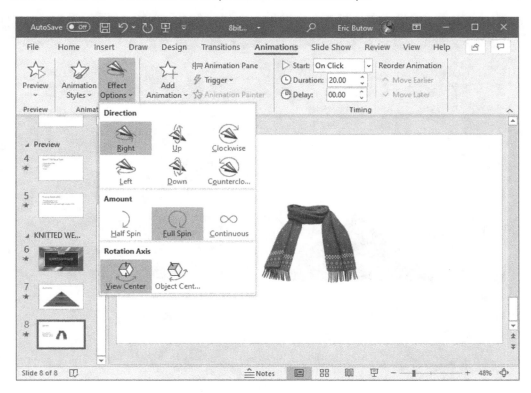

Configuring Animation Effects

When you need to fine-tune your SmartArt animation, you can change the animation effects. Start by clicking the slide in the left pane that contains the SmartArt graphic, and then click the SmartArt graphic in the slide.

In the Advanced Animation section in the Animations ribbon, click Animation Pane. The Animation Pane appears on the right side of the PowerPoint menu. Now click the down arrow to the right of the animation in the list and then select Effect Options from the drop-down menu (see Figure 5.19).

In this example, the Wipe dialog box appears because I applied the Wipe animation pyramid SmartArt graphic earlier in this chapter. Click the SmartArt Animation tab, as shown in Figure 5.20.

FIGURE 5.19   Effect Options menu option

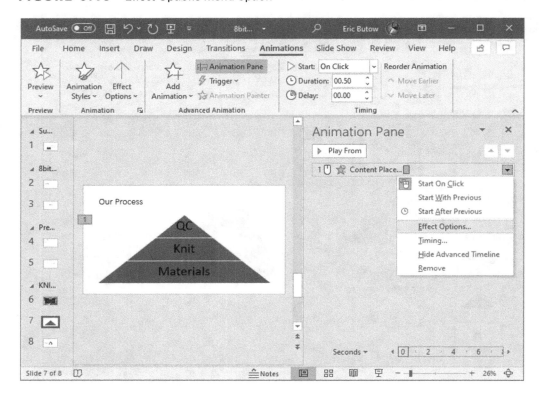

FIGURE 5.20   Wipe dialog box

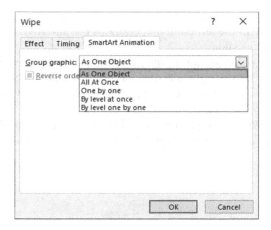

In the Group Graphic section, click the down arrow to the right of the As One Object box. Now you can choose from one of the following sequence options:

As One Object The default option animates the SmartArt graphic as one object. For example, when you use the Wipe animation with a pyramid SmartArt graphic, the first shape grows to its full height before the next shape above or below it grows.

All At Once Animate each shape in the SmartArt graphic at the same time. For example, when you use the Wipe animation with a pyramid SmartArt graphic, all three shapes grow to their full height simultaneously.

One By One Animate each shape individually. When one shape finishes its animation, PowerPoint animates the next shape.

By Level At Once Animate all shapes with the same text level at the same time, starting with level 1. For example, if you have some shapes in a SmartArt graphic with level 1 bulleted text and other shapes with level 2 bulleted text, PowerPoint animates the shapes with level 1 bulleted text first. Once those shapes have been animated, Power-Point animates all of the shapes with level 2 bulleted text.

By Level One By One Animate all shapes with the same text level one after the other, starting with level 1. For example, if you have some shapes in a SmartArt graphic with level 1 bulleted text and other shapes with level 2 bulleted text, PowerPoint animates shapes with level 1 bulleted text one after the other. Once those shapes have been animated, PowerPoint animates all of the shapes with level 2 bulleted text one after the other.

Once you select the option in the list, click OK. PowerPoint previews the new animation effect in the slide.

Differences in Animation Behavior

When you apply an animation style to a SmartArt graphic, pay attention to how PowerPoint applies animation styles:

- When you animate a SmartArt graphic all at once, you will likely find that each shape in the graphic goes at different speeds so that all shapes finish their animations at the same time. When you animate a graphic as one option, the entire graphic animates at the same speed.

- If your graphic has a background, PowerPoint does not animate the background, only the slides.

- If you pick any effect other than As One Object, the background of the graphic will show on your slide when you run the slideshow.

Configuring Animation Paths

If you want to animate a shape so that it appears to follow a path within a slide, such as if you want to have a SmartArt graphic or 3D model move out of the way so that you can display text underneath it, PowerPoint allows you to use two different tools: *motion paths* and *morph*.

Adding a Motion Path

When you want to add a motion path to a SmartArt graphic, follow these steps:

1. Click the slide that contains the SmartArt graphic or 3D model, if necessary. For this example, I will click a pyramid SmartArt graphic.

2. Click the SmartArt graphic in the slide.

3. Click the Animations menu option.

4. In the Animation section in the Animations ribbon, click the More button to the right of the row of transition slides. (The More button looks like a down arrow with a line above it.)

   If your PowerPoint window width is small, click the Animation Styles icon in the Animations ribbon.

5. In the drop-down list, shown in Figure 5.21, click a motion path icon in the Motion Paths section near the bottom of the list. For this example, I'll click Turns.

FIGURE 5.21   The Turns motion path in the drop-down list

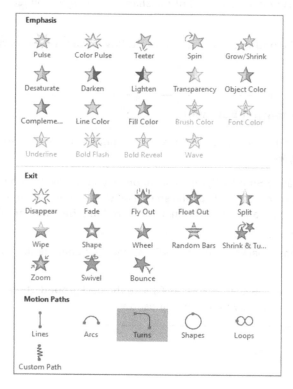

The Turns option icon shows you the path the SmartArt graphic will take—that is, the graphic will move from its current position signified by the green dot and make a turn downward to its ending point on the slide signified by the red dot.

Here are a few important points to remember as you apply a motion path:

- Though Figure 5.21 does not show these colors, they do appear in color on the screen.
- You can draw a custom motion path on the slide by selecting Custom Path from the drop-down menu, as shown in Figure 5.21, but a custom menu path is beyond the purview of the MO-300 exam.
- You can select from more motion paths by clicking More Motion Paths at the bottom of the drop-down menu, as shown in Figure 5.21. This information is not covered in this book or the MO-300 exam.

After you click Turns, PowerPoint previews the SmartArt graphic animation. In this example, the graphic moves to the lower-right area of the slide, and some of the graphic disappears from the slide (see Figure 5.22).

FIGURE 5.22   The truncated graphic in the slide

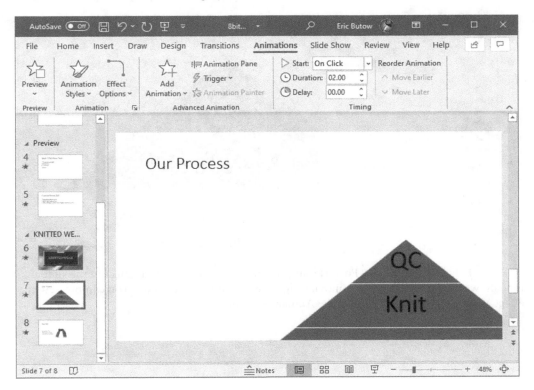

When you start the slideshow and view the slide, click the SmartArt graphic in the slide to move the graphic along the motion path.

Editing a Motion Path

PowerPoint allows you to change the motion path in different directions. Start by clicking the SmartArt graphic in the slide. In the Animation section in the Animations ribbon, click Effect Options.

The drop-down list with a list of options appears, and the options reflect the Turns motion path selected in the previous section (see Figure 5.23).

FIGURE 5.23   Effect Options drop-down menu

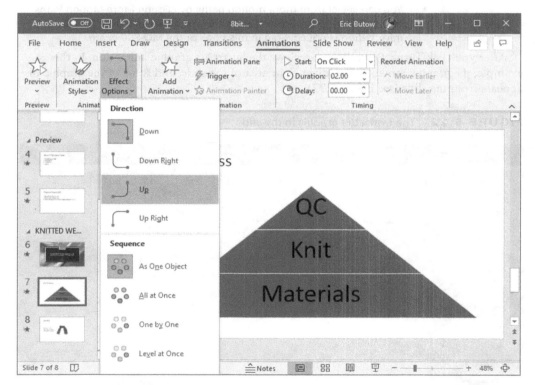

When I click Up in the list, PowerPoint previews the new animation effect in the slide that shows the SmartArt graphic moving right on the slide and then up. You can preview the effect again by clicking Preview in the Animations ribbon.

Creating a Morph Transition

The morph feature allows you to animate an object automatically including a SmartArt graphic, shape, or even text. To do this, you need to duplicate a slide; move the graphic, shape, or text in the duplicated slide to a new location; and then apply the morph transition.

 You cannot use the morph transition to animate a chart.

Create a morph transition by following these steps:

1. In the left pane, click the slide that you want to duplicate. This example uses a slide with text.
2. Click the Home menu option.
3. In the Slides section in the Home ribbon, click New Slide.

    If your PowerPoint window width is small, click the Slides icon in the Home ribbon and then select New Slide from the drop-down menu.
4. Select Duplicate Selected Slides from the drop-down menu, as shown in Figure 5.24.

    The duplicated slide appears in the right pane.

FIGURE 5.24   The Duplicate Selected Slides option

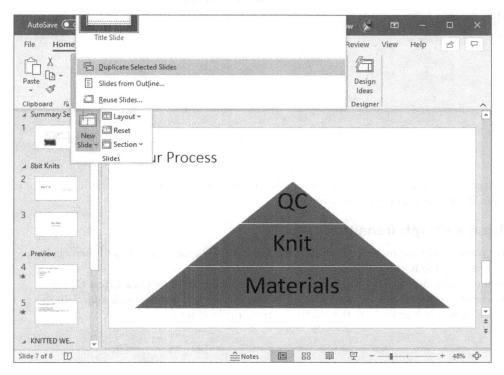

5. Move the text in the duplicated slide to a different location within the slide.

6. Click the Transitions menu option.

7. In the Transition To This Slide section in the Transitions ribbon, click Morph (see Figure 5.25).

FIGURE 5.25   The Morph icon in the ribbon

PowerPoint moves the text from the location in the first slide to the location in the second slide, so it appears that the text is animated.

Editing a Morph Transition

If you want to edit the morph effect, start by clicking the duplicated slide and then clicking the Transitions menu option (if necessary).

In the Transitions To This Slide section in the Transitions ribbon, click Effect Options. The drop-down menu you see depends on the type of morph transition you added. In the example shown in Figure 5.26, the effects are for morphing text.

FIGURE 5.26   Effects drop-down menu

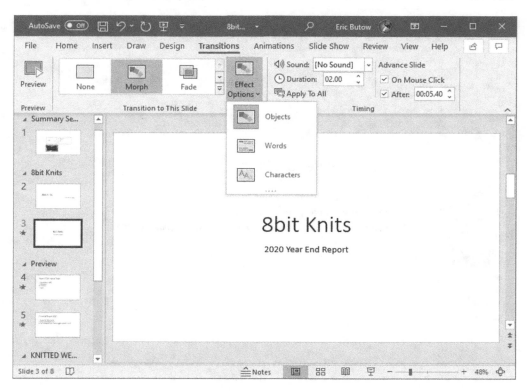

The default option in the menu is to morph the words as objects. You can morph objects and individual words by clicking Words, and you can morph objects and individual letters by clicking Characters. If you morph words or characters, the text in both the original and duplicated slide must have the same capitalization.

Reordering Animations on a Slide

When you have multiple animations on a slide, each marker has a number that tells you which animations will appear in the sequence. You can change the order of the sequence by clicking the animation marker in a slide (see Figure 5.27).

Click the Animations menu option if necessary. In the Timing section in the Animations ribbon, click one of the two options in the Reorder Animation section:

Move Earlier: Move the animation so that it appears earlier in the animation sequence.

Move Later: Move the animation so that it appears later in the sequence.

FIGURE 5.27   Animation marker on the slide

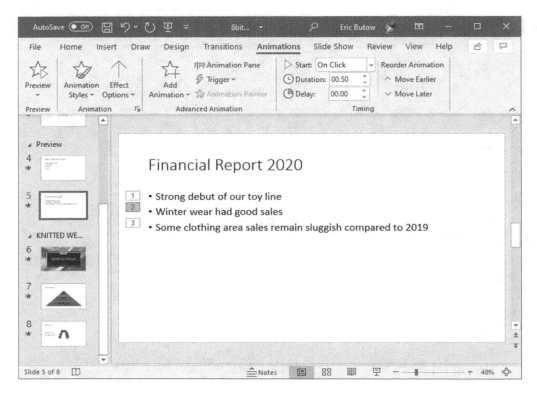

After you click the option, the marker numbers change in the slide. For example, if you move marker 2 to the first animation in the sequence, the number of this marker changes to 1. The marker that formerly had the number 1 changes to number 2.

EXERCISE 5.2

Animating Slide Content

1. Open the slideshow that you created in Exercise 5.1.

2. Add a new slide, which is the third slide in the slideshow, with a Title And Content theme. If you need to know how to add slides, refer to Chapter 2.

3. Add a SmartArt graphic to the content section of the slide.

4. Animate the graphic with the Fly In effect.

5. Add a Turns motion path to the graphic.

6. Change the effect turn direction to Up Right.

7. Add a new slide, which is the fourth slide in the slideshow, with a Title And Content theme.

8. In the content area of the slide, add text and move it to the left side of the slide.

9. Duplicate the fourth slide.

10. In the duplicated slide, move the text to the right side of the slide.

11. Morph the text in the slide.

12. Save the slideshow.

Setting Timing for Transitions

PowerPoint allows you to customize your slide transitions by setting timing, effect, and start and finish options. You can also specify a time to advance to the next slide automatically during your presentation.

Setting Transition Effect Duration

By default, each effect has a default transition time, but if you have not specified a transition the default speed is Auto. Each effect has a different duration.

You can change the duration to a speed you want from within the Transitions ribbon by following these steps:

1. In the left pane, click the slide for which you want to change the transition speed.

2. Click the Transitions menu option.

3. In the Timing section in the Transitions ribbon, click in the Duration box, as shown in Figure 5.28.

   This example uses the Morph transition, so the Duration box shows 02.00, which is the default two-second duration.

4. Press Backspace and then type the number of seconds in the form ss.ff, where *ss* is the number of seconds and *ff* is a fraction of a second, such as 25 for one-quarter of a second.

You can set the duration as precisely as in hundredths of a second. Increase and decrease the duration by 0.25 seconds at a time by clicking the up and down arrows, respectively, to the right of the Duration box.

After you add the duration, you can apply that duration to all of your slide transitions by clicking Apply To All in the Timing section in the Transitions ribbon.

FIGURE 5.28   The Duration box

Configuring Transition Start and Finish Options

PowerPoint lets you advance your slides yourself by default—that is, you can advance to the next slide with just the click of your left mouse button.

However, if you want to change the advancement time for your slide—for example, if you have an unattended slideshow that will loop continuously during a trade show—you can set the transition timing by following these steps:

1. In the left pane, click the slide that contains the transition.

2. Click the Transitions menu option.

3. In the Timing section in the Transitions ribbon, clear the On Mouse Click check box.

4. Select the After check box, as shown in Figure 5.29.

5. Click the time box to the right of the After check box. The default time advancement period is 00:00.00.

6. Press Backspace and then type the number of seconds in the form mm:ss.ff, where *mm* is the number of minutes, *ss* is the number of seconds, and *ff* is a fraction of a second such as 25 for one-quarter of a second.

FIGURE 5.29   After check box in the Transitions ribbon

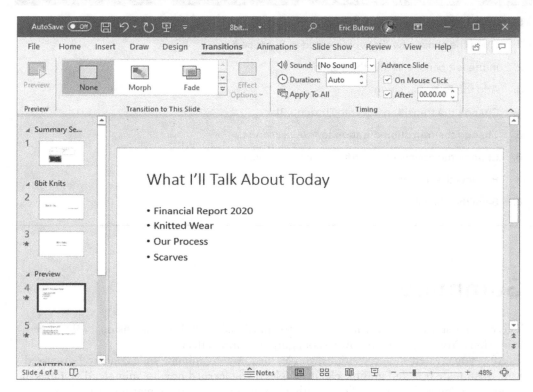

You can set the duration as precisely as in hundredths of a second. Increase and decrease the duration by one second at a time by clicking the up and down arrows, respectively, to the right of the time box.

After you set the time, click Preview at the left side of the Transitions ribbon to see the previous slide and how quickly it transitions to your selected slide.

Keep the following in mind as you configure your start and finish options:

- After you set the advancement time for the current slide, you can apply this time to all slides in your slideshow by clicking Apply To All in the Timing section in the Transitions ribbon.

- You can enable advance timing by using the mouse or automatically by clicking the On Mouse Click and After check boxes. This gives you the flexibility of being able to advance a slide with a left mouse click before PowerPoint advances the slide automatically.

EXERCISE 5.3

Setting Timing for Transitions

1. Open the slideshow that you created in Exercise 5.1.

2. In the left pane, click the third slide.

3. Add the Fade transition.

4. Change the transition effect to Through Black.

5. Change the transition duration to three seconds.

6. Change the advancement After time to six seconds.

7. Preview the transition.

8. Save the slideshow.

Summary

This chapter started by showing you how to apply basic and three-dimensional (3D) slide transitions. You also learned how to configure transition effects.

After you created slide transitions, you learned how to animate slide content. I discussed how to animate text and graphic elements. Next, you learned how to animate 3D models in a slide. I explained how to configure both animation effects and animation paths, and you learned how to reorder animations on a slide.

Finally, you learned how to set the transition effect duration, as well as how to configure transition start and finish options.

Key Terms

3D	motion paths
markers	transitions
morph	

Exam Essentials

Understand how to apply basic and 3D slide transitions.   Know how to open the drop-down list of built-in transition types and apply one to the selected slide.

Know how to configure transition effects.   Understand how to access the list of effects for a transition and apply the effect to a slide.

Understand how to animate text, graphic elements, and 3D models.   Know how to make text appear one line at a time or one letter at a time, animate SmartArt graphics as well as individual shapes within them, animate 3D models, and change 3D model animation effects.

Be able to configure animation effects and paths.   Know how to configure animation effects; configure animation paths, including adding and editing a motion path; and create a morph transition.

Know how to reorder animations on a slide.   Understand how to select an animation marker in the slide and reorder the order of animations.

Understand how to configure transition timing.   Know how to set the transition effect duration as well as start and finish timing options.

Review Questions

1. How do you apply a slide transition to all slides?

   A. A dialog box appears after you add the transition asking you to which slides you wish to apply the transition.

   B. Copy and paste the slide formatting in the Home ribbon.

   C. Click Apply To All in the Transitions ribbon.

   D. Apply the transition in the Slide Master.

2. What ways can you animate text in a slide? (Choose all that apply.)

   A. One word at a time

   B. One letter at a time

   C. One line at a time

   D. One slide at a time

3. After you change the transition duration, how do you see the duration in action?

   A. Click Preview in the Animations ribbon.

   B. Run the slideshow from the current slide in the Slides ribbon.

   C. Click Preview in the Transitions ribbon.

   D. Click Reading view in the View ribbon.

4. What are the three types of slide transitions that you can add? (Choose all that apply.)

   A. Subtle

   B. 3D

   C. Basic

   D. Exciting

5. What menu ribbon do you use to add effects between slides?

   A. Animations

   B. Transitions

   C. Design

   D. View

6. How do you find out how many animations are within the slide? (Choose all that apply.)

   A. Click the Animations menu option.

   B. Click the View menu option.

   C. Look at the marker numbers.

   D. Click the Design menu option.

7. How do you know what a transition effect does?

    A. By right-clicking the transition name

    B. From a description in a tooltip

    C. From the name below the effect icon

    D. By clicking the Help menu option

8. What effect option do you select to animate each shape in a graphic sequentially?

    A. Level One By One

    B. One By One

    C. Size

    D. As One Object

9. What is the default duration for a slide effect?

    A. Auto

    B. Two seconds

    C. It depends on the effect.

    D. Zero seconds

10. What feature do you use to remove an animation from a slide?

    A. The Animations ribbon

    B. The Effect Options icon in the Animations ribbon

    C. The Design ribbon

    D. The Animation Pane

Appendix

Answers to Review Questions

Chapter 1: Creating Presentations

1. A, C. You can change fonts and colors in the slide layout, as well as the title, footers, and effects. You can also hide background graphics.

2. B. PowerPoint automatically displays your slideshow in Normal view.

3. B, D. PowerPoint will print slides 3 through 8, slide 10, and slide 12.

4. C. When you click the Browsed At A Kiosk (Full Screen) button in the Show Type section, the Loop Continuously Until 'Esc' check box is hidden, because when you click the button you loop the presentation automatically.

5. D. Marking a slideshow as final still gives people the ability to edit your slideshow. Adding a password turns off the ability to edit the slideshow to anyone who does not have the password.

6. C. Once you apply changes to a handout master, you will see that all pages in the handout reflect those changes.

7. A, D. Widescreen (16:9) is the default size, but you can also change your slide size to Standard (4:3).

8. B. You can select from one of nine print options for the slideshow handouts.

9. C. The bottom of the left pane tells you what slide you're on and how many slides there are in the presentation.

10. A, C. The default resolution is 1080p, but you can also choose Standard (480p), HD (720p), and Ultra HD (4K).

Chapter 2: Managing Slides

1. C. PowerPoint automatically checks to see if there is more text than a slide can manage and creates one or more additional slides to display the rest of the outline text.

2. B. You still see the hidden slide in the list, but the slide has a gray background and the slide number above the slide has a diagonal line through it.

3. D. When you click Section in the menu, select Add Sections from the drop-down menu to type the name of the new section in the Rename Section dialog box.

4. C. When you select the Keep Source Formatting check box in the Reuse Slides pane, PowerPoint keeps the source formatting.

5. A, C. You can add a gradient and pattern fill to a slide background. The solid fill is selected by default. You can also hide background graphics, but PowerPoint does not classify that as a background fill.

6. D. When you press and hold the Ctrl key as you click each slide, PowerPoint selects all the slides you click on so that you can move the slides to a new location.

7. B. PowerPoint places the new slide directly below the selected slide.

8. A. A page number appears at the right side of the footer, which is the bottom-right corner of the slide.

9. C. Rename the section by clicking the Home menu option. In the Slides area in the Home section, click Section and then select Rename Section from the drop-down menu.

10. D. PowerPoint displays one slide per section within a Summary Zoom slide.

Chapter 3: Inserting and Formatting Text, Shapes, and Images

1. A. To change the format of multiple selections in your document, you must first double-click Format Painter.

2. C. PowerPoint uses the standard blue underlined text for hyperlinks in a slide.

3. C. After you click Picture Effects, you can change an effect in one of the seven effect categories.

4. D. A text box is useful when you want to have text that stands apart from the rest of the text on the slide and that doesn't interfere with the main block of text.

5. C. Selecting Send Backward from the Arrange drop-down list moves the selected object down a level in the stack of objects.

6. B, D. The Place In This Document option is selected by default. Then you have to click the numbered slide that corresponds to the Summary Zoom slide because PowerPoint does not name that slide by default.

7. A. Once you click the Home menu option, you can change the indentation and spacing in the Paragraph section in the Home ribbon.

8. D. After you right-click the shape, select Edit Text from the context menu.

9. B. If you're sharing a slideshow with other people in your company who may not be able to see the graphics in PowerPoint, then Alt text is a great way to tell those people about the messages in your graphics.

10. A, B, D. You can view guides, gridlines, and or rulers by selecting the appropriate check boxes in the View ribbon.

Chapter 4: Inserting Tables, Charts, SmartArt, 3D Models, and Media

1. C. After you move the mouse pointer over Quick Tables, click the table style that you want to place on the page.

2. B. PowerPoint uses columns for the horizontal axis when there are an equal number of columns and rows.

3. A. In the SmartArt Design menu ribbon, click the Reset Graphic icon to clear all your previous changes and return to the original style.

4. C. Clicking and dragging the Rotate icon that appears in the middle of the selected model lets you rotate the 3D model.

5. D. Press the Windows logo key, Shift, and Q at the same time to stop the video recording.

6. A. Both the Table Design and Layout menu options appear at the right side of the row of options in the menu bar.

7. C. A trendline shows you the overall trend of one specific type of data over time.

8. B. When you click the SmartArt icon in the ribbon, the Choose A SmartArt Graphic dialog box opens so that you can select a prebuilt graphic from eight different categories, including the Pyramid category.

9. B, D. You can change the height and width of the 3D model by typing those measurements in inches (and as precisely as hundredths of an inch) in the Height and Width boxes, respectively.

10. D. When you click a bookmark, you can click the bookmark dot in the playback bar timeline to jump to that spot in the audio or video clip.

Chapter 5: Applying Transitions and Animations

1. C. After you apply the transition, click Apply To All in the Timing section in the Transitions ribbon.

2. B, C. You can animate text by specifying that you can animate one letter at a time, one line at a time, or all of the text on the slide as an entire object.

3. C. After you change the duration, click Preview at the left side of the Transitions ribbon to see how long the slide stays on the screen before moving to the next one.

4. A, D. From the drop-down list of transition effects, you can choose effects from the Subtle and Exciting sections, and you can also select from the Dynamic Content section.

5. B. Click the Transitions menu option to add transition effects between slides in the Transitions ribbon.

6. A, C. When you click the Animations menu option, markers appear in the slide and show you the marker numbers in the sequence, with the largest number signifying the last animation in the sequence.

7. B. In the transition effects drop-down list, hover the mouse pointer over the effect icon for a second or two. A tooltip will pop up and tell you what the effect does.

8. B. The One by One sequence animates each shape within a SmartArt graphic. When the animation of the first shape is complete, PowerPoint animates the second shape in the graphic.

9. C. Each effect has its own default duration that you can change in the Transitions ribbon.

10. D. The Animation Pane contains a list of all animations. When you click the down arrow to the right of the animation name in the list, you can remove the animation from the drop-down menu.

Index

Online Test Bank

Register to gain one year of FREE access after activation to the online interactive test bank to help you study for your Microsoft Office Specialist certification exam for PowerPoint—included with your purchase of this book! All of the chapter review questions and the practice tests in this book are included in the online test bank so you can practice in a timed and graded setting.

Register and Access the Online Test Bank

To register your book and get access to the online test bank, follow these steps:

1. Go to bit.ly/SybexTest (this address is case sensitive)!
2. Select your book from the list.
3. Complete the required registration information, including answering the security verification to prove book ownership. You will be emailed a pin code.
4. Follow the directions in the email or go to www.wiley.com/go/sybextestprep.
5. Find your book on that page and click the "Register or Login" link with it. Then enter the pin code you received and click the "Activate PIN" button.
6. On the Create an Account or Login page, enter your username and password, and click Login or, if you don't have an account already, create a new account.
7. At this point, you should be in the test bank site with your new test bank listed at the top of the page. If you do not see it there, please refresh the page or log out and log back in.